Around the Next Bend:
An Adventure in Borneo

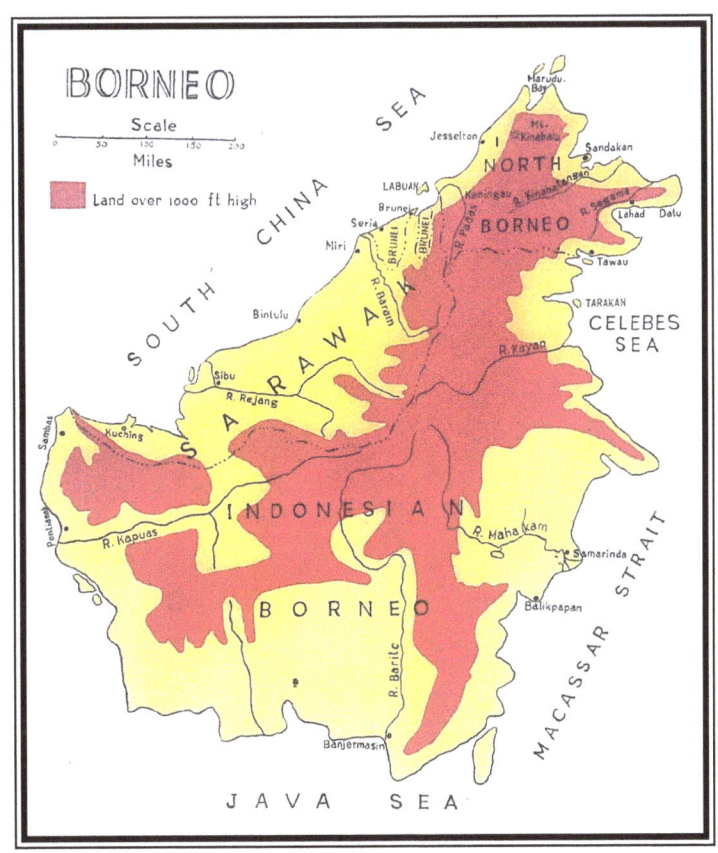

Carol Ann Patterson Boyles-Jernigan

Around the Next Bend: An Adventure in Borneo
Carol Ann Patterson Boyles-Jernigan

Published October 2022
Heirloom Editions
Imprint of Jan-Carol Publishing, Inc.
All rights reserved
Copyright © 2022 Carol Ann Patterson Boyles-Jernigan

This book may not be reproduced in whole or part, in any manner whatsoever without written permission, with the exception of brief quotations within book reviews or articles.

ISBN: 978-1-954978-67-6
Library of Congress Control Number: 2022948120

Jan-Carol Publishing, Inc.
PO Box 701
Johnson City, TN 37605
publisher@jancarolpublishing.com
www.jancarolpublishing.com

My book is dedicated in honor of Brian and Katherine Casidy
and their three sons, wives, and grandchildren:
Mark, Christie, Brendan, Bryce Casidy;
Ian, Kerry, Keegan, Patrick Casidy; and
Blair, Cara, Sydney, Brooke Casidy.

It is also dedicated to my late friends:
Isabel Gamble Curry, Joyce Lawson Hunter and Marie McGrath.

My Tribute

Dottie Wingert Casidy

I authored this book in honor of Dottie Wingert Casidy to celebrate her life. This is my gift to her—the Dottie that I want to remember and knew as a fun-loving, outgoing, vivacious, enthusiastic girl who loved the adventure which she found in Sibu, Sarawak, Borneo. I loved her like a sister. It meant so much to me to relive her experiences as a missionary. I am so sad and angry that my dear friend has contracted this devastating Alzheimer's disease and that she is spending the rest of her life in a care center in Vancouver, British Columbia, Canada not knowing her loving family—husband, sons, grandchildren, and great grandchildren.

I miss her letters and visits, and I pray that someday there will be a cure for her disease. I present her letters from Borneo to you as a tribute to her.

Prologue

This book is an account of Katherine "Dottie" Wingert Casidy's adventures as a missionary teacher in Borneo from 1953 to 1956, where she taught English, reading, Bible and other subjects to hundreds of Malayans and Chinese children at the Methodist Mission School. While there, she lived with headhunters, the high society of Sibu, and met her future husband, Brian Casidy. In the early fifties, Dottie and I were roommates and close friends at Keuka College, located in the Finger Lakes Region of New York State.

I am writing this book for my dear friend as though she was writing it, because she was unable to write her planned account of her experiences in Borneo and now suffers from Alzheimer's disease. I am using the title "Around the Next Bend," because it refers to all the meandering rivers and roads that Dottie encountered during her journey to her destination so far from civilization and throughout her tenure as a missionary. I am using fifty-two letters that she wrote me as a basis of this book, as well as her engagement announcement written by Mrs. Wingert, Dottie's mother, and a letter from our college friend, Joyce Lawson Hunter. In this way I can connect with Dottie as co-author of this book, as she is no longer able herself to meaningfully communicate.

At the time Dottie made her decision to travel 9,522 miles to Sibu, a primitive town in the wilderness of Sarawak on the island of Borneo, I agreed with her other friends. We felt this vivacious girl, with so many achievements, was throwing away her opportunities, but Dottie had majored in Christian Education, and we knew she felt being a missionary was her calling. This book is a celebration of my friend's life, and I get the privilege of helping her share her life in Borneo, which she is now unable to do.

Table of Contents

Chapter 1: Katherine "Dottie" Wingert 1

Chapter 2: Journey to Borneo 3

Chapter 3: "Li Ling" 15

Chapter 4: Impressions of Borneo 19

Chapter 5: Methodist Mission School 26

Chapter 6: Social Life 33

Chapter 7: The Engagement 41

Photographs 44

Chapter 8: The Wedding 50

Chapter 9: The Honeymoon 56

Chapter 10: Married Life in Sibu 58

Chapter 11: Singapore, Malaysia 63

Chapter 12: The Singapore Riots 66

Chapter 13: Return to America 70

Epilogue 73

Resources 76

Acknowledgments 77

About the Author 78

Chapter 1

Katherine "Dottie" M. Wingert

Katherine was always known as "Dottie," distinguished by her beaming smile. She was a bubbling, enthusiastic, vivacious girl with a love for adventure. When her neighbor, Mrs. Petrie, saw her for the first time, she called her "a little dot." Hence, her nickname Dot or Dottie. I never knew her as "Katherine."

Dottie grew up in Elmira, New York, the oldest child of Mr. and Mrs. Laban Wingert. Her father was a district manager of a J. J. Newberry, an American five and dime store chain in the 20th century, who died on November 1, 1950. Her younger brothers are Randall and Laban. When grown, Ran, as he was called, worked for an airline, and Laban was an architect.

I met Dottie when we were both students at Keuka College, then a women's college, now co-ed, in upstate New York located three miles from Penn Yan on Keuka Lake.

Dottie was petite in stature—5'1" tall with dark hair and brown eyes that sparkled when she talked. She majored in Christian Education, and I in French and Latin. We never met until the beginning of our junior year when her roommate, a nursing major, left campus to begin her clinicals in area hospitals, and my roommate, Isabel Gamble, won the Norton Scholarship to study abroad at the University of Edinburgh in Scotland. Dottie and I became roommates at Strong Hall, the cooperative dormitory, where all the residents earned part of their tuition by sharing the household duties of waiting on table, cooking meals and performing other related chores. It was located on the shores of Keuka Lake about ½ mile from the main campus. On class days we rode the milk truck to Hegeman Hall, standing on the running board singing, "On My Merry Oldsmobile."

This was a new experience for Dottie, as she had been living in Ball Hall, a residence on campus.

Dottie and I had such fun being roommates. I even got used to her setting the alarm for 3 a.m. so she could attend her birding class. I was going to miss her as my roommate senior year, as I had promised Isabel that I would room with her on her return from Scotland. Nevertheless, she and I remained the best of friends for over 69 years. During our senior year, as we were contemplating our futures, I was hired by the College President to remain at the college as an Admissions Officer for three years.

Dottie, unknown to her friends that she wanted to be a missionary, had applied to the Methodist Mission Board for such an experience. Her college friends thought she was crazy to want to leave the United States to work in a foreign country when she had so many attributes to find another kind of position closer to home. However, Dottie was always looking for an adventure. This is her story told in her own words.

Keuka College Graduation,
Penn Yan, New York, in 1953

Chapter 2

Journey to Borneo

Missionary Orientation

I always wanted to be a missionary, so in the middle of my senior year at Keuka College, I applied to the Methodist Mission Board and was accepted, much to the chagrin of my classmates. Upon graduation in June 1953, I attended a six-week summer session at the Hartford Seminary Foundation in Hartford, Connecticut to prepare for my career as a missionary in Borneo.

At the Seminary, I attended classes in Evangelism and the Malayan language. I gained experience in witnessing to prospective church members, in conducting vesper services and morning devotions, and I learned that Borneo was the third largest island in the world. Finally, I completed all necessary procedures required for my trip to Borneo.

Upon completion of my studies, my family saw me off to New York City where I boarded the Dutch freighter, the "MS Tabinta," which would make six stops between Halifax, Nova Scotia and Penang, Malaysia. It would take three more boat trips, adding up to a two-month journey, to reach Sibu, Sarawak, Borneo in Malaysia.

The Trip to New York City

On Sunday morning around 7 a.m. on September 13, 1953, my mother, Mrs. Schaff, daughter Martha, my brothers Ran and Laban, and I drove from Elmira, New York to

New York City. We made good time until we arrived in Wurtsburg in the Catskills, where traffic was bumper to bumper driving into New York City. We finally reached the Prince George Hotel at 3:15 p.m. where we had reservations. This visit to New York City was the same as always, trying to see as much as possible in the shortest amount of time. We got tickets to the Radio-TV show, "Firestone Hour," and saw the movie, "Roman Holiday," at Radio City Music Hall.

September 14, 1953 – Brooklyn, NY

On Tuesday afternoon, we took about an hour's taxi ride to Pier 3 in Brooklyn. When we arrived at the ship, Ran and Laban investigated every little place in the freighter. When it was time to leave, I walked down to the end of the long pier and said "goodbye" to everyone.

Sailing on the "MS Tabinta"

My friends from Hartford Seminary, Ellen Atkinson, Carol Lee Little, Marge Hooper, and I boarded the 23-year-old Dutch freighter, the "MS Tabinta," in the late afternoon. Ellen and I were traveling to Sibu, Sarawak, Carol Lee to Penang, and Marge to Ipoh. Before sailing, we settled in our cabin where we had two bunk beds for the four of us. I pressed my silk polka dot dress to wear to a four-course dinner at the captain's table, where we were impressed with the elaborate place settings of fine china and glasses made in Sweden and waiters who were small men from Java, one of the islands of the Greater Sunda Islands in Indonesia. They were dressed in blue and white striped jackets and velvet caps. The ship's officers were wearing white dress uniforms.

At dinner, we were surprised to learn that our first stop would be Halifax, Nova Scotia as we had expected to sail directly to Alexandria, Egypt. We also found that the captain liked to venture a little, so that we might see things we would not see on another ship. Around 7:15 p.m., the ship was hooked to two tugboats, taking it out into the Atlantic Ocean where we saw the Manhattan skyline fade away and the Statue of Liberty wave goodbye. We watched the moon set and the Long Island shoreline disappear. By 10 p.m., we were asleep inside our cabin when we were suddenly awakened by an electrical storm rocking our ship. In the morning, the ship's officers were quite surprised to see us for breakfast, as no one else on board appeared. Breakfast was a little different—cheese, liverwurst, all bran nut bread, and coffee. We were hoping to have something different the next day—maybe eggs and toast as we really got hungry on-board ship. In between meals, we were only served coffee.

After breakfast, Ellen and I sat on the deck, knitting and talking until lunch time. I wanted to finish a brown sweater that I had been knitting for my brother Laban, so I could mail it to him from Halifax.

Ellen, Dot, Carol Lee, and Marge sailing on the "MS Tabinta."

September 17, 1953 – Heading for Halifax, Nova Scotia

The four of us girls were keeping our heads above water. We were not seasick yet. At dinner that evening, we learned that a hurricane was headed toward us. The captain was hoping it would reach Halifax before it hit us. Right now, we were in a thick fog, so every few minutes the fog horns were blowing, and the ship was rocking. To prevent seasickness, Ellen passed around a bottle of pills and glasses of water to each of us.

Another startling piece of news from the captain was, we might change ships because the Arabian government wanted the "MS Tabinta" to carry Muslim pilgrims back to their countries. If that happened, there would be over 600 passengers aboard, and it wasn't advisable to have four girls on board ship at that time. We arrived in Halifax late on September 17th and sailed from there the next day.

After we left the Port in Halifax, we sailed to the Mediterranean Sea seeing the African Coast on the way. I put on my bathing suit, so when we reached Alexandria, I would be ready for a swim. On board ship, Ellen and I brushed up on our Malayan language. The officers and crew spoke it, so we thought we wouldn't sound so green by the time we reached Singapore. We expected to have a teacher in Sibu to instruct us in this language.

I couldn't believe that I was really on my way to Borneo. The ship was very pleasant; I could really sleep, which I needed badly. I wrote letters, knitted, and read. It was quite the life, and I was getting paid for it!

September 23, 1953 – In the Azores

I wrote this letter to my mother about my experiences in Halifax:

"We had a wonderful time in Halifax. The weather was beautiful, cool, and clear. The coastline of Nova Scotia reminded me of the rock formations along the Maine coast by Eastport. Halifax is a large city, but the only industry is fishing, and did it smell! T. Eaton and Company, Ltd. is located there, not as large a store as the one we visited in Montreal. Did buy some British yarn, a sketching pad, and charcoal pencils. We stopped in an old antique shop that had some lovely things like dishes and furniture. It certainly would be a very pleasant place for a summer vacation.

The bay where we docked was very picturesque, and I tried to do a few charcoal drawings, but they don't resemble the bay at all. I'm going to draw a setting at each port where we land; we'll have some good laughs when I get back home.

Saturday was a rough sailing day, but the sun shone and we saw four other ships. Ellen and I read and knitted most of the day, and we played cards with the captain in the evening. Sunday was a very peaceful day, listening to records and a church service. In the afternoon, the officers played deck games with us. In the evening, Marge and I taught the captain to play the card game called canasta. He seemed quite young, maybe in his middle 40s with flashing eyes, very tall and slender, blonde hair, and when he laughed, he looked like he was thinking up something devilish to say. My card playing partner was the lead steward who was in his late 20s and married. We discovered that the officers wore their white dress uniforms every evening, and their Bermuda shorts and white knee socks, the rest of the day. At the captain's dinner, we ate by candlelight, everyone dressed up and sometimes we had steak or smoked eel, but the first course was always soup. I'm saving some of the menus to send home to you. On Monday, we survived another rough storm, making everyone seasick except me, which I think forgoing breakfast saved me. About 9:30 a.m., we came back to the cabin, took seasick pills, and slept until supper time. The captain was quite proud of me to be the only passenger for lunch. The storm was so bad that the ship's crew put metal discs in all the portholes, but before they did that, Ellen was in bed, half asleep, when a wave came in the window soaking her bed. It happened so fast that it made us laugh all morning. The Java men, the waiters from Indonesia, came into our cabin laughing, and in a few minutes that incident was the talk of the ship. Carol Lee, feeling a little better, drew some typical watercolor portraits of each of us. Ellen's was the best—green in the face. Tuesday, we spent the whole day on deck, except for an hour that I spent washing my clothes in the shower where we had the only hot water. When we washed our clothes in there, we took showers afterwards. Then we hung our wet pants, etc. on strings all over our cabin.

Yesterday of all days, about four men, who decided to set up an aerial for me so I could play my radio, were in and out of our cabin all morning dodging the wet clothes. One of the tubes had burnt out in my radio, and the men said I couldn't get the tube in Alexandria. They insisted that my mother could send me some. The Chief Engineer and I had become good friends. He was married, about 55-60, so no worries. I told him that I didn't expect to receive any packages from home, and he just laughed, saying he got packages every month from home. I told him he was just spoiled. These men were only home eighteen days out of a year, and sometimes it might be over a year. Their leaves were based on three days a month after the first three months out of home port. They said the "MS Tabinta" sailed from Holland to Houston, New Orleans, Jacksonville, and up to New York to meet us. After it reached Singapore, it might be in the Pacific for a year sailing between San Francisco and Java. These men sure had tales to tell.

The Chief Engineer was in a Japanese prison camp during World War II. The officer that I ate with was in a convoy between England and North America, traveling along the very extreme northern part of the Atlantic where they got a lot of storms. All the officers, with whom we had made a big hit, said they would supply the ice cream if we would make them apple pies. They were surprised that we girls weren't nuns wearing dark, black robes and stockings instead of dressing in jeans and heavy shirts to keep warm. Yesterday, we wanted cokes, and just about dinner time, the Java men came in with four glasses of cokes and when we had finished, they brought us four more bottles to our cabin and a box of Holland Chocolates from the captain. By this time, the dinner gongs had rung, so we took lollipops that Ellen had bought in Baltimore and gave one to each officer.

One of our pet phrases around here is, "There's never a dull moment." I can't possibly record all the little things that happened on board ship, but one incident about the captain's cat happened one early morning. She was about to have kittens but the captain didn't want her in his cabin, so he put her in ours. There was a little hole in the wall next to the floor, so when they washed the cabin, the water would run out. Well, one night the cat got in that hole without our knowing it. About 2 a.m. in the morning, she tried to get out by climbing up our screen door and meowing. What a sound, especially in the middle of the night! She climbed up and sat on the ledge over the door. Ellen, Marge, and I tried to get her down, but she hissed and meowed continually so we couldn't sleep. At 2:50 a.m., Carol Lee's dander was up so she put a blanket over her head and knocked the cat down, and she didn't come out of that hole.

About 6 p.m. one evening, we passed south of the Azores, which are nine islands 800 miles off the coast of Portugal, so we went up to the bridge to observe them.

About 10:30 a.m. the next morning, we passed the Flores Islands off the coast of Portugal, which were in the western group of Azores. Then, we went through the south-side of Gibraltar; the half-moon was bright enough to see the side with the huge rock. The previous night there was a full moon, and it was just like daylight outside; the water was very calm.

There were so many things, Mother, I would have liked to say to you before I left, but I couldn't find the words. Thanks for being so patient with me. I really caused everyone a pain in the neck trying to get ready for my trip. I guess life in Elmira has calmed down to normal. For some reason, I can't say 517 West Church Street is home because I've only been there on holidays and weekends when I was home from college. I guess I think of 661 Grove as home where we lived during my high school days. It's wonderful to get home, but youth are always on the go. I hope you will forgive me for being such a wander bug. I love you very much and appreciate everything you did for me. I realize how important it is to thank people every day for what they have done. It's the little things in life that count. If we keep each other in our prayers, we will be ever so close, and when I get home from Borneo, I'll have all sorts of stories to tell. Take care of yourself and say hello to all for me.

With all my love, your daughter."

October 2, 1953 – Alexandria, Egypt

About 6 a.m. Friday morning, before entering the Port of Alexandria, we had engine trouble, so we were on pins and needles all day looking towards the City of Alexandria until it got fixed. Two fellows, who were supposed to leave the ship, couldn't go ashore. We had been up since 5 a.m., so it had been a long day to wait to see the sights of Alexandria.

When we arrived in port around 8:30 p.m., all kinds of police with little red hats and black tassels came aboard telling the captain that no one could go ashore until the next morning because we were illegally anchored in the harbor. The shipping company agent had forgotten to notify the officials of our arrival. I wanted to go to Cairo to see the pyramids and meet the ship at Port Said, but the other girls didn't like the idea, and the captain didn't want me to go by myself. Latif, one of the passengers who was getting off in Egypt, became a good friend, who offered to take me to Cairo and show me around, but the captain still advised me not to go. So, we went through customs, and what a mess. The Egyptian government was a bottleneck for trouble. Latif paid $160 in customs duty for a radio, tape recording machine, and camera.

Latif and we girls took the treadways (buses and trolley cars) to the beautiful beaches and saw all the very wealthy homes of Europeans and Egyptian government officials.

Alexandria, the largest city on the Mediterranean Sea, was very modern in an ancient environment with telephones, buses, a few good roads, movie houses, and cars from all over the world. Everyone lived in apartment houses, which were very modern and beautiful, but the people in the native section of the city were poor. There were little kids and women with small babies in their arms begging for money.

There were so many things that I learned about Egypt that I didn't have time to record. It was interesting to be with Egyptians who spoke English, since all the people we ran into spoke Arabic. We ate ice cream in a small café, which reminded me of one of the streets in Paris that I had visited. Then, we had lunch in a very quaint place, saw two palaces of the former king, walked down the native streets, and saw men sitting around smoking their water pipes and small children and women begging for money with tears in their eyes so they could have food. The filth and dirt in the native section was terrible and very smelly. We ate dinner in a beautiful hotel and then took a buggy ride to the downtown business area.

We were going to visit some friends of Latif's about 9 p.m., but I told him we better get back to the ship, which was planning to leave at midnight. We took a taxi out to the pier, which was about three miles. We were very much on edge because the first gate was closed, but the drawbridge wouldn't come down until 1:30 a.m. At the next gate, the same story, but at the third gate we got in where we had to reveal everything that was in our bags.

While standing there, we heard the "MS Tabinta's" whistle, which meant it was leaving. With sore feet from wearing heels all day, we ran about ¼ mile over cobblestone roads to get to the ship, for if it had left us, we would have been in a terrible predicament, as the police had our passports. When we left the ship, all we had was a piece of paper saying we could go ashore for the time the ship was in Alexandria.

October 4, 1953 – Port Said, Egypt

Port Said (pronounced SAYEED) was a busy seaport situated on the northern entrance of the Suez Canal. After we read our mail, we went ashore where I bought an ivory inlaid wooden plate and earrings. While in Alexandria, Latif, the Egyptian fellow, had bought me some ivory earrings, a box of Turkish Delight (candy made of honey and nuts), two ivory bookmarks and a silver pin.

At midnight, we were in a convoy of ten ships about 180 miles long going through the Suez Canal. Late in the morning, we anchored at the second lake in the canal to wait for the convoy from the south to pass. While anchored, we all jumped overboard for a swim in the Suez. When I dove from the side of the ship, I received a funny sensation hitting the water, as I had opened my eyes in salty water. The lake was rough, so with salt water in my eyes and mouth, I didn't last long swimming. The rest of the afternoon, I sat in the sun taking pictures of the countryside.

I hated the hot and sticky climate. There was dirt in the air and millions of sticking and biting flies all around. I always appreciated the letters I received. It's quite funny, but being out of the country away from family and friends, it made me appreciate the little things. Every American, if they could afford it, should see the suffering, starvation, and dirty politics being played in the world. What I have seen of the world is enough to make your hair stand on end.

October 7, 1953 – In the Red Sea

The Red Sea was a seawater inlet of the Indian Ocean lying between Africa and Asia. When I arrived in Jeddah, the second largest city and seaport in Saudia Arabia, no one was allowed to go ashore because it was a Muslim holy site. We couldn't do much in the extreme heat, as it was so hot, I had to sleep outside my cabin on the third deck. The men were unloading flour and cleaning off the decks to receive 599 Muslim pilgrims from Indonesia and Malaysia who had traveled to the Hajj in Mecca.

As the "MS Tabinta" had no accommodations other than the two already occupied cabins, the Muslims were loaded into the "tween decks" of the ship where they lived for four weeks or so before they arrived home in Southeast Asia. The ship did not stop again until Northern Sumatra, the town of Belawan near Medan where most of the pilgrims got off. I wrote this letter to my mother and Laban:

"I received a letter from Carol Ann, one in Port Said, which took five days from the States, and the other at Jeddah, which took seven days. I hope to catch up on my letter writing while in port for a few days. Our trip in the Mediterranean was delightful. The water was so smooth, and the sun so warm that you thought you were on land because the ship was not rocking. It was warm enough to go without a jacket, and in the evening, we went up on the ship's bridge to watch the moon appear, to study the stars, and watch the ships and tankers go by of which 75% were from Jeddah. We passed Malta, saw Sicily in the far distance, passed the Rock of Gilbraltar at midnight, and stayed up almost all night to see the coastline of Spain and North Africa."

October 25, 1953 – Penang, Malaysia

We arrived in Penang early Sunday morning, leaving the "MS Tabinta" around 9:30 a.m. We went directly to the church where everyone was in tears to learn the minister was leaving to return to the States for medical care.

After dinner, Ellen, Carol Lee, and I toured Penang. We walked in the jungle, fed the monkeys, picked wild orchids, took pictures, saw the beautiful white beaches, and visited a Hindu temple. Afterwards, we attended the Senior Methodist Youth Fellowship (MYF). Later, we settled Carol Lee in her new home where she had a huge bedroom and private bath. All the homes had their living rooms on the second floor and their bedrooms on the first floor. Ellen and I spent the night at the minister's home under a huge mosquito net.

Monday morning, we enjoyed a wonderful American pancake breakfast followed by chapel at the Anglo-Chinese Girls' School. Afterwards we took a grand tour of the mission's classrooms, which had French doors (no windows) with vents that were opened during classes. The rooms were 30' x 30', well lighted and ventilated, which seated around 40 pupils who wore green uniforms.

October 26, 1953 – Taiping, Malaysia

We left Penang around 2:30 p.m. by car arriving in Taiping at 5:30 p.m. amongst beautiful mountains and visited an outstanding girls' school. The trip from Penang was beautiful, thrilling, but hot. We saw rubber plantations, tin mines, people taking baths in a muddy creek flowing by the side of the road, coconut trees, bananas growing wild, monkeys, and oil refineries. Since supper was never served until 8 p.m., we took a scenic drive. The sunset was out of this world. In many sections of this part of the world, the lawns were kept looking beautiful and everyone enjoyed the parks. We saw all kinds of plant life, rain trees, Royal and Coconut Palm trees, Tulip trees, Rubber and Bamboo trees, and flowering vines.

On October 28, 1953, Ellen, Marge, and I drove to Sitiawan. The next day, we were in Ipoh where Marge Hooper was to be the missionary. On October 31, we traveled from Ipoh by train to Kuala Lumpur and on November 3, to Malacca (now Melaka), and then we left by bus on November 4 to Singapore where Ellen and I stayed for two days on November 5 and 6.

At Kuala Lumpur, I had a Keuka reunion with Elsie Gan and Vivian Kang, who took me to Elsie's parents' house for "High Tea." Her parents spoke Cantonese, so Vivian interpreted for us. She was teaching geography, hygiene, English, and science in the Methodist Girls School at which the principal was a Methodist missionary.

The "Rajah Brooke"

On November 7, Ellen and I sailed on the "Rajah Brooke" from Singapore to Kuching, Sarawak. After two full weeks in Malaysia, our trip from Singapore was wonderful and restful. To recap our busy two weeks, we got off the "MS Tabinta" in Penang, drove to

Taiping, Sitiawan, Ipoh and took a train to Kuala Lumpur and Malacca, and a bus to Singapore. Our expenses for the two weeks for transportation, room, and board all came to $80.00 in American money.

Our ship, anchored about seven miles down river from Kuching, the capital of Sarawak, was not sailing into Kuching until the tide came in at 6 p.m., so we took a taxi to Kuching to meet Annie Pittman at a guest house, one of the missionaries that we would live with in Sibu. When she arrived, she couldn't believe that we were finally in Borneo. After registering with the Colonial Government, we had tea with the treasurer of the Sarawak colony. A government official took us through customs which went very smoothly, as we didn't have to open our luggage. We paid only a $7.90 duty fee in American money for a radio, cameras, new clothes, and other materials. Afterwards, we did a bit of sightseeing.

The "Meluan" and Chinese Launch

On November 10, 1953, Ellen, Annie, and I boarded the "Meluan" and on November 11, we changed to a Chinese launch on the Rejang River to sail to Sibu, Sarawak where on November 14, we were met by the mission staff. Ellen and I were on the "MS Tabinta" about seven weeks from New York City to Penang, Malaysia. It was another 17 days before we arrived in Sibu, after traveling the length of Malaysia, spending time in Singapore and then taking the "Rajah Brooke" to Kuching, the "Meluan," and a Chinese launch to Sibu.

"Rajah Brooke"

Chapter 3

"Li Ling"

In Sibu, located in the westerly part of Borneo in Sarawak, was "Li Ling," the name of my new home. It was a huge, spacious, brown, two-story building located in jungle-like surroundings. The house was open with screened windows including the ground floor, which had a few rooms for the servants who were cooks and housekeepers, two offices, and a guest room. The first floor was upstairs, which had a huge living room with bamboo furniture, and off that room was a dining room. Opposite the dining room was a balcony with stairs up to three rooms, where Ellen, Martha, the last termer, and I had our 18' x 18' bedrooms with baths. Two sides of my room had screened windows with shutters that guarded against the rain. The third side had a full-length closet with shelves, and the fourth side had a door leading into the bathroom. I felt lost in such a large room. I lived with Ellen, Martha Graf, Annie Pittman, and later two older missionaries ready to retire.

When I finally got unpacked, clothes hung, hooks put on the shelves, and odds and ends put away, I wrote to Carol Ann and my mother letting them know that I could use some good American soap, soft toilet paper, Jell-O, light reading material, pocketbooks or small magazines, and any kind of food stuffs. All goods were very expensive because they came from England. My radio, that had a tube burnt out on the "MS Tabinta," was finally replaced so I could listen to the BBC and Manila, but I couldn't reach the United States.

On Thanksgiving Day, two bishops, who had arrived from the New York City Methodist Mission Board and 14 missionaries ate Thanksgiving dinner with us at "Li Ling."

I made a mince pie and two pumpkin pies using a native golden pumpkin. The menu included chicken, peas, mashed potatoes, and salad. Ellen and I made place cards using paper napkin holders with a turkey on a ring on which we printed each person's name. We also made paper Pilgrim hat nut cups for each dinner place.

Later that week, the bishops sailed down river to baptize some Dayaks who had become Christians. They were really interested in learning about Christianity. I told them, before entering a Dayak home, they would have to take off their shoes and sit on the floor, and the women would have to sit by themselves on one side of the floor.

On December 20, 1953, I wrote to Carol Ann that I wouldn't receive any Christmas packages to open this year as my mother's package hadn't arrived yet. I thought maybe it would come on the "Meluan," but if it didn't arrive for Christmas, I would open it on my birthday on January 4.

The mail situation was strange. On December 17, I had received a letter mailed from Elmira on November 30. Most of the air mail arrived in eight to twelve days. I finally learned a secret about mailing letters to the States. If I mailed a letter on a Tuesday or Friday, it would reach Singapore the next day, catching the "Comet" into London in three days and then it would go to the States. Mail came from all different directions. I received a bird calendar from Elmira stamped San Francisco. Carol Ann had difficulty mailing things to Sarawak. I wrote her that most people just wrote Borneo instead of Sarawak on their envelopes, which made it confusing to the postman.

Christmas week was busy with committee meetings, decorating the house, baking tons of cookies, and buying presents. On Christmas day, all of us missionaries woke up at our usual time of 6:30 a.m. We sang a few carols with our servants' children and gave them gifts. At 9 a.m., Ellen and I rode our bikes to the church service where we met a very pleasant Englishman about 27 years old among the Chinese congregation. After church, we wished "Merry Christmas" to practically everyone in Sibu. Madeline, a missionary wife, told Ellen and I that we had a note and telephone call from some man, who sounded like our friend Southby with whom we had played badminton. We were in 7th heaven. When we arrived home, we found the note was from Bill Southby inviting us to a Christmas luncheon, which we couldn't attend because Annie, Louis Dennis (the head missionary of Sarawak), Ellen, and I were going to Bawang Assan to baptize 80 Sea Dyaks to celebrate their becoming Christians. Bill was quite crushed that we couldn't accept his invitation.

Bawang Assan was about 16 miles from Sibu. It was an extremely primitive place where 24 families lived in a longhouse built on stilts about 10 feet high with bamboo slab flooring. Each family had one room without electricity, plumbing, and the only evidence of western culture was when the men wore short pants and shirts on dress occasions. When we arrived at Bawang Assan, we were given a royal reception of firecrackers which were used for all kinds of celebrations. China provides the world with firecrackers.

Here is where I saw my first Dayak regatta, which reminded me of Keuka's crew races in the spring and the boat races on Seneca Lake. That afternoon and evening we visited over 30 families, praying, and reading scriptures to each family and feasting. By 9:30 p.m., we attended a talent show put on by the teenagers. Radio, movies, and especially American movies were interesting to them. That night Ellen and I slept on the bamboo slat floor, and we were so sore on awakening. The "john" was a crack in the floor, which I wouldn't use, so I was happy to get home late in the evening.

My mother's package finally arrived five days after Christmas. In her box were some books from Carol Ann, which I shared with Jenny Harris, who lived upriver and loved to read, so I shipped any new books to her first, but I kept "Keys of the Kingdom" to read myself.

I was simply thrilled opening Carol Ann's package with all the little gifts wrapped so neatly. Since Christmas wrapping paper was scare in Sibu, I took everything apart carefully to save it for future use. I opened the peanuts immediately. I didn't have to pay anything at customs, which was unusual for the men not to open my package.

On New Year's Day, I helped the cook bake gingerbread and for dinner we ate veal, potatoes, native squash, and Iban greens, which were leaves off a small tree. I worked in the kitchen when I was not busy doing something else.

On New Year's Eve, we sat around talking until midnight and then we retired to bed. We had fun in the afternoon when Martha took all of us missionaries on a ride in her 30' Chris Craft.

On January 26, 1954, I wrote Carol Ann that a wonderful thing happened recently when the "Keukonian" arrived. What a thrill to open this newsletter to digest all the articles and to know the people and that place. Being in a foreign country, living with people whose customs and manners were far from what you practiced, really was a good lesson for anybody, especially those living in the United States. I'm not preaching about everyone taking up their stakes in the States, but the people living in the United States should be more appreciative of where they live. I mention it so much because I took most everything for granted, and I'm really finding life exciting doing without things. Once in a while, though, I like a change.

When Annie Pittman injured her knee, I became responsible for planning the meals, buying the food, and paying the bills along with my teaching responsibilities. Ellen did an excellent job taking over the hostel. Annie improved rapidly after surgery. Her knee knitted well and in 8 to 10 days the pin in the knee came out.

My friends and I ate many meals outside "Li Ling." I learned to eat Chinese food, even pig's stomach. All our food was prepared by the cooks either in a soup or sauce to cover up the terrible taste.

On March 23, 1954, I wrote Carol Ann, "I'm so glad you had an opportunity to see my family again. So glad to hear that you enjoyed the log of my trip on the "MS Tabinta." Someday, I would like to put Borneo's experiences into words. If I ever do, the title will be "Around the Next Bend" referring to all the crooked turns in the rivers and roads."

I had my appendix removed in Singapore in October 1954. When I arrived back in Sibu, two more missionaries had moved into "Li Ling": Emma Palm, an elderly nurse, and Martha McCutcheon, an old China missionary, both on their last term. The residents changed frequently. Emma later moved to a small settlement near Sibu called Sungel Mera. Annie Pittman returned to the United States to retire.

The house was not as quiet as it used to be. I had moved downstairs to the basement, but I didn't sleep there because it was flooded with eight inches of water. At low tide, the water went out, but the drainage wasn't good. My teakwood desk and all my wood furniture were water stained.

"Li Ling," Dottie's residence

Chapter 4

Impressions of Borneo

I was disappointed to see how dirty the surroundings were in Sibu. It was hot and sticky everywhere. By noon, the temperature was in the 90s, and I was covered with sweat. I had to go home from school, take off my clothes, put on a T-shirt and skirt and usually take two showers between 1 p.m. and 6 p.m.

The roads were rough, sandy, and holey on which to ride my bike. In 1953, there were only 107 miles of paved roads in the whole of Sarawak with another 63 miles of gravel road, so the only way one could travel was by boat on the Rejang River or by air. Most cities were "around the bend" on a crooked river. The rainfall averaged between 180-225 inches a year as it rained daily, and water was everywhere. The road to the airport, where my friends and I went swimming in an old bomb crater, was a mixture of mud and stone. Even the airstrip was a mixture of grass and gravel, which was built by the Japanese at the end of WWII. After the Japanese left in 1945, the bomb craters on the runway were filled in, but some, which were a distance from the runway, were left, and that is where I swam. There were no swimming pools in Sibu in 1952-1956.

During my first year, I discovered Sibu was part of a British colony—a small agriculture community of less than 10,000 people (in 2017, the population was 168,000), yet it was the second largest city in Sarawak. Its population was mixed, predominantly Chinese with Indians, Malays, tribal groups forming small minorities and about 50 Europeans, who were Australians, New Zealanders, Americans, and Dutch. There were two national groups in Borneo, the Ibans and Dayaks. The Ibans, who were headhunters, were the largest, making up 34% of the Sarawak population.

Sarawak was divided into five divisions, with a government officer in charge called a Resident. Each division was made up of several districts with their own officers.

I learned the following information about Sibu from the "1954 Sarawak Annual Report": "Sarawak is in the westerly part of Borneo where Sibu is located. It is very mountainous with the highest peak being Mt. Murud at about 8,000 feet. From the North, the Rejang River which runs through Sibu is one of the transportation routes that flows into the South China Sea. The many waterways are the major lifelines of Sarawak. All human and commercial travel depends upon the rivers. Sea-going vessels can reach Sibu, Simaggang, and Kuching to take major trade. Here is a wide expand of flat land relieved occasionally by hills. Much of it is swamp, mangrove or nipah palm, rich in minor produce. These areas are inhabited by the Malays, Melanus, Chinese, and Sea Dayaks. There are great tracks of virgin jungle that are uninhabited and unknown except to small bands of nomatic Punans who live on animals and plants."

I discovered the Rejang River, which was made up of many streams, was the lifeblood of the town, making Sibu a commercial center. Boats went up the Rejang into places like Kanowit, Song, and Kapit daily with passengers and cargo. There were no roads out of Sibu, so all travel was either by water or, once a day, a DC3 plane went north to Miri, Labuan, Jessleton, and other towns. The southbound flight went to Sarawak's capital, Kuching and to Singapore.

The hill tribes people—Dayaks, Kayans, Kelabits, Penans, Ibans, and others—periodically visited Sibu from way up the river. It was interesting to see them proud and stately, the men in loincloth and bare feet, the women naked to the waist. They wandered around town completely untroubled by the stir that they were creating. Many of the men had tattoos on their throats, shoulders, and hands.

The Chinese ran most of the independent businesses, with a few Indian shop owners, while the Malays primarily formed the clerical and domestic staff. There were two rather grubby cinemas showing old movies, one store importing frozen food from Singapore and many stores catering to the population mix. There was a large meat and vegetable market with a covered roof but open on all four sides and one gas pump.

Along the river, there were makeshift jetties for the various types of river craft, the Customs Warehouse, the main docks for the ocean-going ships, the courthouse and judicial offices, the Island Club and the Residency, where the chief government officer for the Third Division lived in solitary bachelor splendor. Most of the homes for other government department heads were in the general area, and the small hospital was close by.

Because of Sibu's proximity to the equator, the days were pretty much the same length year around with darkness coming between 6 and 7 in the evening. The humidity was terrible and affected everything. If I left my shoes in the closet without heat or light, they would be covered in mold after a week.

The area around Sibu was very flat, low-lying, subject to flooding, and could be very depressing at times to me because I was accustomed to the rolling hills and lakes of New York State. Sometimes the people had to go to work or school by boat instead of walking. I found that the people in Sibu were nice, which made up for my first impressions. The road to town was picturesque. I saw Chinese, Malay houses, and Dayak longhouse residences. There were bamboo hedges, little Chinese children, ducks, and chickens running across my path as I rode my bike with my Gibbon, a monkey, wound around my leg.

From a trip Ellen and I took to Kapit, a city about 90 miles and twelve hours away from Sibu, I bought an eight-week-old Gibbon, who I named Mittie. She was a monkey without a tail that walked like a human on its two hind feet. She clung to me constantly, so I took her riding with me on my bike wherever I went. Mittie chewed everything she could get her hands on, and later she destroyed the clothes in my closet and died from eating a roll of toilet paper.

On this same trip, Ellen and I boarded a Chinese launch, which was smaller than a tugboat. It stopped whenever and wherever anyone wanted to get off. It carried everything: pigs, chickens, freight, and if room, people. It reminded me of the Greyhound buses in the States stopping at every little farmhouse and railroad crossing. It was unusual to have white people travel on Chinese launches, so all sorts of unfamiliar things happened. The people, who spoke about eight different dialects of Chinese, Malay, and Dayak, touched the material of a dress or a man could be seen cleaning his ears.

At Kapit and further up the river, the Methodists worked with educating the Dayaks. At a town beyond Kapit, there was only jungle, a river, church, and students attending a school.

From this trip, I also bought a Kenyah war shield and a beautiful bamboo rug. The Kenyahs live far from the coast up the big rivers of the Third and Fourth Divisions. They build fine longhouses and strong boats.

I received an article on Sarawak from my Elmira friend, Byron, that appeared in the November 28, 1953 "New Yorker" magazine. In it, the author, Alan Moorehead, wrote about his impressions which, in a letter to my mother, I compared my impressions with his.

The author wrote, "Sarawak is a wonderful place which I agree." (In Agnes Newton Keith's book, "White Man Returns," who lives in North Borneo, describes Sibu: "Forgotten are its handsome, lazy log-packed river, and shady shore, its prosperous spicy pepper vines, its green-scum swamps, its flower-scented nights, its children, women, and men of good will.") I hope that in the future I could display a picture of Sibu, showing its beauty as the land of enchantment.

In the article, Alan mentioned no Communists or, at any rate, no open Communists. This is partly true because the Communists were influencing the youth in Sibu as they did when they moved into China. Alan writes of the "Rajah Brooke," the "pleasant little ship that leaves Singapore in the afternoon and reaches Kuching three mornings later" was an experience that I also had. I, too, experienced the picturesque view of looking out the porthole and seeing, "The bright green jungle coming down to the water's edge, with just a clearing here and there around a thatched native village. Coconuts, uprooted tree trunks, and enormous jelly fish floating by on the outgoing tide, and Malayan sampans (flat-bottomed Chinese and Malay wooden boats) dotting about between the ship and the shore."

The short history the author gave was good, and it was helpful to me because I was teaching Sarawak history to the 6th grade. I happened to buy a complete history of Sarawak written by the late Rajah, but it was so detailed about facts of the early life back in 600–1800 A.D.

The author pointed out that he liked the Land Dayaks, but I liked the Sea Dayaks, which I think are like the Land Dayaks in the construction of their homes, superstitions, food and eating habits, dress and raising crops. The Sea Dayaks differed in that they used boats as a means of transportation, and the Land Dayaks traveled by foot. The Sea Dayaks boats are called longboats for they were about 25 ft long and 2 ft wide. Most of the boats have Johnson Seahorse, Mercury, or Evinrude outboard motors. The Sea Dayaks living near Sibu have the advantage of buying Western products, such as oil lamps and outboard motors.

One of the first things that hit me smack in the face about the Dayaks, was the way they painted their teeth. Alan said they painted their front teeth with a little square of red, green, or yellow enamel and some had inlaid gold placed between their teeth that gave a striped affect. Not only did they have this enamel or gold on their teeth, but they chewed beten nuts that stained their teeth red.

The author seemed to me quite conscious of the Dayaks nakedness as I did at first. It seemed so strange to see them almost naked, except wearing loincloths around their middle, but after a while, it seemed natural, for the cloth was expensive. I could feel with the author his experience of seeing these people and them seeing him for the first time.

When it was my birthday, I wanted to do something different, so Ellen and I took off on our bikes for an all-day ride into the jungle. Here we learned what the author meant about the silence of the jungle. At noon, when the sun was penetrating in "the onion soupy mud," the heat and humidity were just terrible; nothing was stirring, we sat for a while trying to hear something move, but nothing did. The trail was like the one the author took, full of holes with lots of roots and mud. Fortunately, we had our own food, so we didn't depend on the food supply that the jungle produced. I'm afraid, if we depended on the jungle for food, I wouldn't have found anything—not even a coconut.

No one ever told me about the elaborate ceremony drinking TUAK, the whitish cloudy fluid made of fermented rice, which was sweet and sick to the taste, but I'm glad. I ate the sticky, spiced rice that was packed into long tubes of palm leaves, but I didn't care for that either.

We did have an elaborate ceremony when the Dayaks, who were headhunters, and lived in that village of over 12 longhouses, like the ones the Native Americans lived in the States, turned from their superstitions to Christianity. The longhouses were designed with an open covered communal area in front with individual rooms on the back. The communal area had slatted floors that had openings between the floorboards, so excess food could be stuffed through the cracks to feed the chickens and pigs below. Sometimes longhouses were 80 rooms long, built above the river on stilts about 10 feet from the ground because of the damp weather. I even had the experience of sleeping with them on their straw mats woven by the women. The one superstition, leaving a light on all night to keep the evil spirts away, had not left this tribe.

There is one thing that Mr. Moorehead saw and experienced that I didn't see, was the tattooing of a girl. I thought one time of having a tattoo placed on my hand, but since this article, I'm not going through the pain that girl experienced.

Ellen and I took a trip on the "Meluan" up the Rejang River. We had taken this small freighter when we came to Sibu last November. We were bitten by insects in the middle of the night, so in the morning we changed to a ship at Sarikei. However, we discovered that we couldn't disembark until 6 p.m. at the very time we were expected to attend a dinner party. So, instead we took a small launch, and what a ride! We reached out and touched the jungle leaves and picked beautiful flowers as we went by. All kinds of sights were on the launch—Dayaks with tattoos on their necks, arms, back, wearing only loincloths to cover their bodies, Chinese mothers breastfeeding their children, and Malayans with red teeth.

During Easter vacation, which began on April 22, 1954, Ellen and I took a trip to Simanggang, the main town in the Second Division located between Kuching and Sibu. To get to Simanggang, we had to fly to Kuching, which took 45 minutes from Sibu. It was Ellen's first plane ride. After 20 minutes in the air, we could see almost to the Indonesian border, the coast, and the mountains upriver from Sibu. The China Sea looked like a smooth, glassy pond. Then to reach Simanggang, we had to board a boat, the "Pussi," at the airport, which means "Wooden Pigeon" in English. It was a government launch with a crew of five Malays, about 64' long with sleeping accommodations for six. Since we couldn't make the trip in one day, our boat pulled into a small sea fishing village where we spent the night aboard sleeping on deck, as we tried to swat the mosquitoes away to prevent prickly heat sores.

The next day we were on the "Pussi" until 5 p.m. and during that time, I got a beautiful tan from wearing a sundress that made my back almost black. When we arrived in Simanggang, I noticed lovely rolling hills and beautiful shade trees. In Sibu, there were hardly any trees along the town's streets, and it was so hot when the sun beat down.

Simanggang was a small town of Dayaks and only a handful of Europeans lived here. The Dayaks in this area were more prosperous than in the Third Division. Their homes were kept up, their children looked healthier, and their diet was better than the majority of Dayaks for they raised cattle. In other parts of Sarawak, the Dayaks raised their own rice paddies, chickens, and pigs. When I wrote to Carol Ann, I told her, "I guess you think I am lost in the wilds of Borneo because I haven't written you in several months."

Ellen and I visited a newly married couple, who were stationed in Sibu for a year, when the husband was transferred to the hospital here as head doctor. We were treated royally by the Resident, a government officer in charge of the division, who invited us for drinks. The next day we were invited to a curry lunch to which our hostess invited a group of Europeans for cocktails. Here we met a young lawyer, who the next day took Ellen and me up the Lange River where he stayed, and we took the launch back to Simanggang. During that time, we were three hours walk from the Indonesian border. From the mountains, we could see Sarawak and Indonesia. The next day we took a Chinese government launch from Simanggang to spend the weekend in Kuching. Ellen and I were the only white people on it from 8:30 a.m. until 7:30 p.m., so we sat in the sun, observed the scenery, read for a while, and I got a tremendous burn on my legs.

While in Kuching, I bought some beautiful silk, sarong Dayak style material with silver and gold thread in the pattern to make some cocktail dresses and a sundress. One lot was a regal purple with silver design, and the other lot was a reddish-rust plaid with gold thread running through it.

Ellen and I spent the night on the launch, so we arrived at the airport in plenty of time to catch our flight back to Sibu. It was a very rough ride with lots of air pockets. When we landed at the airport, we discovered Sibu was flooded, and our friends had to go through four feet of water to meet us.

Our Easter vacation was wonderful. I had never experienced anything like it in my life.

Another experience that I had was traveling to Sarikei with Louis Dennis, the head missionary of Sarawak, in his Johnson Seahorse Motorboat. Sarikei, noted for its pineapples, was a small town located on the Rejang River where the river empties into the South China Sea. After our visit with the local leaders, we left Sarikei at 4:30 p.m. with the tide against us, so it took us longer than three hours to return to Sibu. About 6:15 p.m., we ran into a terrible rainstorm with driving winds which soaked my clothes from head to toe, as I had only a raincoat and blanket to protect me. During the rainstorm, our driver drove so close to an incoming launch that we could see the peoples' faces; he missed crashing into the boat by a hair. The river was dangerous at night due to floating logs. It was dark when we arrived home in Sibu.

Chapter 5

The Methodist Mission School

Ellen Atkinson and I were hired to teach in the new Methodist Mission School in Sibu and to provide religious education to the youth and the community. Two weeks of our long trip, prior to arriving in Sibu, was visiting many of the Methodist Mission Schools in Malaysia to observe their methods of education. This experience would benefit us when we began teaching in Sarawak. These schools were in Penang, Taiping, Sitiawan, Ipoh, Kuala Lumpur, Malacca, and Singapore.

At the Sarawak Annual Conference in December 1953, I was appointed to teach classes in the morning in the English Primary School, officially known as the Hoover Memorial School, and in the afternoon to devote my time working in religious education with the youth in the district. There were two departments in the Hoover Memorial School. English had its school in the morning, and Chinese in the afternoon. Doug Coole, a Methodist missionary, was the principal over these departments, of which each had a dean. Hoover Memorial was located downtown on Island Road not far from the Island Club. Behind the club, was the Rejang River from which very cool breezes blew into my second-floor classroom. The school buildings were much different from the ones in my hometown. Since there wasn't a heating problem, the windows didn't have glass. The school building had two stories with concrete walks outside the building, which provided protection from the children's muddy feet because it rained almost daily. There were three rooms on each floor. On the second floor, there were two balconies that were the length of the building on both sides, with doors across from each other opened for cross ventilation. Six windows made the rooms light and airy. The 6th grade was my homeroom, but I taught 4th, 5th, and 6th graders in age from 12 to 19 in oral English, reading, composition, geography, and sometimes history or nature study. Most students completed their middle school education in the Chinese school, which was equal to junior high in the States. This was the highest grade they could attend, after which they registered in the 6th grade in the English Department to improve their English. I refused to teach those students who were wizzes in math because they could add huge columns of figures in a matter of minutes. They were also competent in geometry, algebra, and trigonometry. I felt that it was going to be difficult to teach English to such a varied group of older students who needed lots of instruction, as well as teach children ages 12 to 14, who were more advanced in English because of their previous enrollment in the English school.

I discovered that my job might be more than teaching in the elementary school, as a college for ministers was being organized to begin in January, and they wanted Ellen and me to teach a class there. I invited Carol Ann to come to Borneo to help me teach in the college.

I became concerned about my many responsibilities, as I was an advisor to the Conference, the District, and I worked with the youth in Sarawak and throughout Malaysia in developing the Methodist Youth Fellowship (MYF). There were over 100 Chinese, Malays and Ibans, who joined the local MYF. It was a challenge to work with them as each spoke a different language. Some spoke Mandarin, some Foochow, some Cantonese, and Malay and some could understand English. To be an active MYF member, the youth had to participate in one of the following activities: evangelistic work, teach in church school or set up Sunday Schools in outlying communities. Also, I was expected to attend the Women's Society functions, learn Mandarin and continue to study Malay. I wondered when I would have time to study and prepare for my classes. When they discovered I could play the piano, I was expected to play for church services, teach piano and play for the Christmas pageants. In addition, I was appointed English secretary of the Hostel Advisory Committee, assigned three Sundays to spend time with each church, work with the choir and church school.

On January 14, 1954, several days before the new term began on January 17th, the principal asked me to register students for the new year, by receiving the 6th grade students' tuition of $8.00 a month and their school supply money. I felt that students in the

States were fortunate to have free education from kindergarten through high school. In Sibu, students paid a monthly tuition, so if their performance was poor, and they were advised not to return to school, no refunds were made. When school started in January, I taught my classes in the morning, and I normally slept a part of the afternoon as it was so hot. Sometimes I prepared my lessons and gave at least one piano lesson. I started giving piano lessons to eight students on Monday and Tuesday from 3 to 5 p.m., and I played the piano at chapel on Tuesday mornings at 9:30 a.m. Sometimes I led chapel with a singing session and asked the congregation to express their thoughts on certain topics. I really enjoyed my oral English classes in Grades 5th and 6th.

In my music classes, I taught "Itsy Bitsy Spider" and the "Farmer in the Dell." The children didn't play games at recess because the teachers said it was too hot. Marbles was the popular game, which very few girls played. The Chinese custom was for girls to be very passive and quiet. When there was an English drill in the classroom, the girls would never say a word. One week the school was hectic as the 5th grade teacher had been sick with typhoid fever. I had to teach both 5th and 6th grades at the same time, but finally a fellow in high school took over the class permanently without any formal education to teach. That was a major problem in Sibu.

One day in 1954, I was in the teacher's room looking out the window onto the main street of Sibu where I saw quite a few people that I knew. When I needed something to do, I would take off on my bike, ride down to the pier and talk to many of the custom men. I became great friends with the captain of the pilot boat, a Malay, who always wore a beaming smile. At noon, when I left school, if I had a load of books in my arms, he helped me by putting them on his motorcycle and taking them to the road where I turned into "Li Ling." Another friend was a Sikh, who wore a white turban around his head as his hair was never cut. He was a police officer, No. 179, so every time I saw him, I said, "Hello, 179." I didn't know his name, but he got the biggest charge out of my calling him "179."

One Friday, a group of teachers and I rode our bikes on a rough, crooked, and scary path into the jungles about ten miles where people lived far away in the rubber plantations and pepper gardens to observe a Chinese school. On a Sunday, Ellen and I rode our bikes to a new village built on stilts to speak to the children in a church school. About ¼ mile, we rode on banks about three feet wide, three feet off the ground with water and mud below, two-way traffic on foot and people riding bikes. I was so scared that I would fall; I took a deep breath and pedaled my bike. When I saw another bike riding towards me, I closed my eyes and passed him. It reminded me how I would close my eyes when I drove my mother's car into the garage at home with hardly room to breathe.

In May of 1954, I couldn't believe that I had been in Sibu for over six months, as the weeks went by so fast. I had been so busy at school with Religious Emphasis Week, meetings, and entertaining the Press Secretary from the American Embassy in Singapore. He never said why he was in Sibu, but I thought it was because of the French, Indo China situation which was quite serious. The Communist influence grew stronger every day in Sibu, taking Sarawak by subversion. The high school students liked Communism, and we sat with our hands tied, as those with Communistic ideas were hard to manage. The students said the school belonged to them, so they could control what happened in the classroom. Even in my 6th grade, there were signs of Communist sympathizers. One of the worst things we faced, which was not easy to stomach, was the Communist ideas of some of the churches' strong lay workers. However, I enjoyed my teaching because I did have students who were willing to learn, but I was discontented when their eagerness for learning ceased. When the governor visited three schools in Sibu, it was a hectic day teaching and attending teas in his honor.

One day in school I thought my little ones, the 5th graders, were so cute, but pests. They talked and carried on, so I called the dean to come into my classroom. It was near the end of the school year, so what made me so mad was two boys jumped from their seats and went home. When they returned, they had to apologize to me in front of all the students, which meant "losing face" to the Chinese students.

In October 1954, I flew to Singapore to have my appendix removed by an American doctor at the Youngberg Memorial Hospital. When I returned to Sibu, I felt well enough to return to teaching, but a member of the District Office didn't want me to return to school for another two weeks, but I felt fine, so I twisted his little finger. He insisted that I remain in my seat to teach, which was against all that I had ever learned about teaching. When report cards came out, I was busy giving tests, correcting papers, and averaging the grades to distribute the reports.

Beginning November 1, 1954, I started a strict diet to lose 20 pounds as my American doctor in Singapore said that I must lose weight. He said it was hard on my heart to be fat in a tropical climate. I took vitamin pills along with my food, which made me feel so much better, because for a month I could never get enough sleep to keep my eyes open in my morning classes. I weighed every Sunday to see if I had lost any fat. My doctor told me I had grown two inches, which I found hard to believe. I was so surprised when November seemed to arrive so soon. It was hard to believe that Ellen and I had been in this tropical country just north of the equator almost one year. The weather was miserable, and it was the rainy season. The rain would stop for about ten or twenty minutes and then it would start again. At lunchtime, it would rain so hard that I refused to leave school until 2 p.m.

On November 15, 1954, Ellen and I celebrated a whole year's teaching in Sibu by inviting Eda Mamara, a teacher from Sumatra, Judy Tan, our Chinese friend, and Brian, our English friend, to a spaghetti dinner in Ellen's room at the hostel, and then we attended a program presented by the English Department at the high school. My boss, Dr. Clara French from the Methodist Mission Board, also came for a visit. She had written me a great deal about her visit to Keuka and Elmira. She said Carol Ann was a very charming girl, and she was so glad to have met my college roommate. I had a big dinner party for her on Friday and on Saturday, Ellen and Martha took her upriver to visit the Dayaks. The next day she returned to visit the Sibu area. On Tuesday, I took a day off from school and took her to Bawang Assan to see an Iban settlement of nine longhouses dating from the 18th Century. On the next Saturday afternoon, Dr. French, Ellen and I rode bikes across the river to explore the gardens that supplied fresh vegetables to the Sibu market and discovered a new ferry which crossed the Rejang River.

It was quite a year, as my students usually learned only the 3R's, but I tried all sorts of things to get them interested in news and other world events. I wondered if they really digested all the information I gave them. My students corresponded with other children of the world and discovered a favorite hobby of collecting stamps. The formation of the Boy Scouts and Girl Guides made a big difference in developing their personalities, which affected their attitudes toward other people in and outside the classroom. Their leaders were effective, as they taught the boys and girls to learn the laws and how to put them into practice. It was thrilling to see how scouting promoted the working together of Malays, Dayaks, and Chinese.

One weekend, Lord Llewellyn, a Boy Scout executive, arrived from Singapore to review our program, so our scouts gave him a reception on Sunday night and a campfire on Monday night. Life in Sibu continued with all sorts of interesting things happening.

When I gave my 6th graders reading tests, I would get so discouraged because I had to give them poor marks for not reading carefully. I had just three scholars out of 38 students in the class. There was one student that I hoped would either go to work or leave school, as she refused to do the dictation on many days. What could a teacher do?

School closed the end of November and finals began on December 1. Afterwards, we started to plan our Christmas programs. Due to my appendix surgery in October, I was two weeks late in administering my tests. When report cards came out, I was busy giving tests, correcting, averaging, and marking them.

I really used the camping books with my Girl Guides that Carol Ann sent me. They had exercises to help them with their second-class tests. I promised the girls that I would take them hiking and camping on our Christmas vacation, which usually began on December 7 for one month. Before doing that, I made reservations to go to Kuching to spend a few days shopping before flying back to Sibu. The two beautiful purple orchids that I bought in Simanggang last Easter vacation were in full bloom, so I planned to mail them to my mother for Christmas.

I planned other trips to visit my friend Connie in Binatang (now known as Bintangor), and travel to Sarikei, Tanjong Mani, and Kapit. Ellen went to Singapore to visit her friends and vacation in the mountains. Judy, one of our teachers, and I were thinking about going to Singapore and Siam on our vacation next June. It was hopeless to go to Burma (now Myanmar) as visas were difficult to get unless Lillian, a college friend, could pull strings on her end. Elsie was back in Malaysia, so I hoped Vivian Kang and Fran, my roommate at Hartford, would come to Sibu in July and August for their summer vacation.

The airplane rates to fly between Sibu and Singapore had been reduced to $140 Straits money. I invited Carol Ann to spend Christmas with me in my lovely tropical isle in the South China Sea. I wrote her, "There's no place like it; thank heaven." I spent my second Christmas, as I did my first, with the Dayaks at Bawang Assan who had been Christians for two years. Their ideas were a little different from Americans. They were very respectful and reverent in the spirit in which they did their celebrations.

The Chinese New Year called "Hari Raya," was celebrated on January 3, 4, 5, 1955. It was a public holiday for which the Malays were excused from school, so only a handful of Chinese were in my classes. All night long, the Malay men were at their mosque worshiping. Many times, I wished that I had a tape recorder to record their weird to me sounds. For four days, the Malays led up to this great event by lighting firecrackers. At sundown, they would light candles and place them along their wooden plank walks that led to the streets. It was a very picturesque sight that reminded me of the States at Christmas when lights are placed outdoors. "Li Ling" was located right in the Malay kampung (village), the mosque was on the left and the cemetery was lighted. Each grave had candles around it to keep the evil spirits away. No one called on the Malays during this time because they would have to follow their customs. After January 5, it was important for friends to visit and take food, hot orange drinks or American crème soda. Since most of my students were Malays, I had quite a few visits to make.

In 1954 and 1955, my social life increased, and my activities limited the time I had to write letters.

Elementary school, Sibu

Chapter 6

Social Life

When I knew I was going to Sibu, I didn't think there would be any social life outside the mission group. However, I discovered some good-looking Englishmen wandering around Sibu in their white Bermuda shorts, white knit socks, and white shirts. Most of them were bachelors between the ages 25-40, working for the Borneo Company Ltd. (like the Hudson Bay Company). They traded with the natives in rubber, hardwood, pepper, rice, and their handiwork. Unless we had formal introductions, Ellen and I couldn't speak to them—only smile. I was introduced to a Mr. Lionel Storrs, the local manager of the Straits Steamship Company, who invited me to take a trip up the Rejang River with his crew, which I thought I would accept, since school didn't begin until January 17, 1954.

One Thursday night after dinner, I had gone upstairs to change clothes and when I came down, a young gentleman, Bill Southby, was sitting in a chair. After introductions, we carried on a conversation for 1½ hours. He was from England and had been working for the Borneo Company Ltd. in Sibu for two years. He asked Ellen and me if we played badminton, so later we bought badminton rackets to play with him. He concluded by asking us if we would like to go to the movies and to his place for tea, so I thought, *Maybe we are on the road for an exciting three years, as there are about 15 good-looking unmarried men around here who lived about ¼ mile beyond "Li Ling."*

I saw my first movie in Sibu one Thursday, and one of the shorts pictured was about the alligator farm in St. Augustine, Florida, which made me feel right at home. My aunt's brother-in-law managed this attraction. It was so good to hear American dialect and see

American cars. Although the main movie was in Chinese, a friend translated for Ellen and me. The acting was good, much better than the third-rate movies in the USA. I was really corrupting Ellen, who hadn't been to an American movie in eight years, but she was willing to attend in Sibu because there wasn't anything else to do. That evening of all evenings when Ellen and I were out, the Englishmen called to invite us to a party at their residence on Sunday. We were unable to attend, as I had a speaking engagement in the country, and Ellen had to teach a Sunday School class.

On February 6, 1954, I wrote Carol Ann, "What a life I'm having here in Sarawak." On New Year's Eve, Polly and Doug Coole invited Ellen and me and two bachelor friends to dinner. One didn't appear, but Bill Southby did as well as a Dr. and Mrs. Stewart. Bill asked Ellen and me if we were doing anything Wednesday night. I was attending a dinner party, but not Ellen, so he asked her to go swimming. A very wealthy "Chinese man" invited me, all the important government men of the 3rd Division, the judge of Sarawak, about 25 English people including three bachelors to a dinner. I had the good fortune to sit with Peter, a person I had been trying to locate to fix my radio ever since my arrival in Sibu. He was the spitting image of my friend, Bob Phillips, 28, in Elmira, and he had traveled all over the world. This dinner was my debut to meet the English, and I didn't arrive home until 12:30 a.m. The next day, Dr. and Mrs. Stewart invited Ellen, Bill, and me to a picnic and an all-day swim in clear, cool water in a bomb crater at the airport. Bill was simply a doll. They invited us, sunburned and sleepy to their home for dinner at 8 o'clock and recommended us to become members of the Island Club. Hopefully, we could join if the dues weren't too steep.

One day in February 1954, I heard from the missionaries that an English-speaking man called at "Li Ling" to see me when I was downtown. He left a message that he would see me that evening. I wondered if that was when Brian Casidy contacted me? He doesn't remember the exact date he met me, but he related the following incident to me: "We had one grocery store in Sibu, Kim Guam Siang, which sold frozen meat, vegetables, and fruit flown in from Singapore, and it was where all the 'Europeans' shopped. I was in there one day when Dot and Ellen came in as I was leaving. I wanted to introduce myself, but I didn't know what to say. I was so shy that I finally blurted out, 'I don't think you will find any Virginia Hams here,' and I quickly exited the store." He said this was probably in February 1954, and he must have introduced himself later, but he only remembers the goofy encounter above.

During February 1954, Bill Southby provided lots of social life for Ellen and me, inviting us to the Island Club to dances and other activities. "Life in Borneo could be exciting." We went on moonlight swims, picnics, car rides, dances, dining, and so many other things. The fellows there were dolls, but they really needed to be more outgoing with women.

One Sunday Bill picked Ellen and me up at 2 p.m. in his English jeep, a Land Rover, to go to the swimming hole, but it was so crowded we decided to eat lunch. On the way to find a place to eat, it started raining, so we pulled into a small clearing until it stopped. It was rather late, around 3:30 p.m., so we cooked hamburgers. Afterwards, we climbed the only hill in the area. When we reached the top, we were so hot that we laid down and took a nap. That evening I had to speak at church. Luckily, I had already prepared my talk. Afterwards, Bill and Ellen picked me up to go swimming. About halfway home around 11:30 p.m., Bill's car stopped and wouldn't restart. He was gone for over an hour to get one of the fellows to drive his motorcycle to where we were located at midnight to protect us from any men who might have surrounded us. It was 1:30 a.m. by the time Ellen and I arrived home. Bill took a lot of ribbing from his housemates about having two girls in his car. One evening Ellen and I went bowling at the Island Club, where we played three games with Bill and several club members. We had a wonderful time except for one person. A fellow, named Tony Mann, thought he was the only man on earth. He was only 26, very good-looking, blonde, but extremely stuck on himself. He drank whiskey and soda all the time and constantly smoked, even while swimming with a cigarette holder in his hand or mouth.

One night after prayer meeting, Ellen and I were invited to dinner at the doctor's house for a farewell party for the doctor who was leaving Sibu, and a welcome party for the newly arrived doctor. The English ate so late, around 9 p.m. Our mothers, the older missionaries who lived with us, thought it was terrible at all the gadding around we were doing and for eating so late. They really took us over the coals. If they only knew that Ellen and I had joined the Island Club, I guess our names would have been mud.

One week, I spoke at church, chapel, MYF, taught classes, corrected papers, and had a little social life, which made it difficult to find time to write and follow a set schedule. I really thought this new life was good for me, as it got my mind off the problems of missionary life—the difficulty of living with older missionaries and teaching such a diverse group of students. Before I left Hartford, we were told it would be difficult living with older missionaries, but I didn't believe it was true. My life really got quite exciting and interesting in late February and March 1954 when I started dating Brian Casidy, a Rugby player, who was 6'2" tall with reddish blonde hair and extremely good-looking. He owned a motorcycle and quite often you could see us riding into the jungle or going swimming. I really fell for him in more ways than one. Brian was also attracted to me for my beaming smiles and other attributes. He was always coming over late to "Li Ling," making himself at home cooking bacon, eggs, pancakes, or whatever he felt like.

Brian was hired March 1952 in London, England to work for one of the largest timber companies in Great Britain—Montague L. Meyer Ltd. In October of that same year, he was asked if he would like to work in their operations in Sarawak where they had a forest concession, sawmill, and office. Each of these facilities were 3½ hours away from each other by longboat on the Rejang River. Brian was interested so he moved to Sarawak in December 1952. When Brian left to go down river to supervise the loading of lumber on a South African cargo vessel, he brought me his record collection. Ellen had bought a three-speed record player, so we could enjoy his records. When Brian returned, I invited him to dinner, so we could listen to his records all evening. He liked classical music.

When Peter and I went out to dinner one evening, he mentioned the fact that I was Brian's girl. I guess Brian had made it clear with the bachelors in Sibu that I was his girl. I paid no attention to Brian's desires. I continued to go out with some of the bachelors such as Tony, a psych problem, who drank heavily because he lacked something to do. If I could help him in any way, I wanted to do so; he was really a nice fellow. I knew Carol Ann would like Brian; he didn't smoke and only drank beer with the fellows. Ellen and I had an expression calling each other jelly fish because we weakened when our fellows came around. Ellen had dated Bill Southby frequently, but he left in March for England permanently so she was lost without him, but there were other bachelors she could date.

Every time Brian and I went swimming, I took my camera, but I never got around to taking any pictures. One Sunday, we were all going swimming, but Ted, another bachelor who worked in a timber mill, got the bright idea to go upriver to the Borneo Company's lumber mill. So, at 2:30 p.m. he picked Ellen and me up, and we worked for two hours in the pouring rain unsuccessfully to get his Johnson Outboard Motor to work. Afterwards, we went to Brian's house, where the fellows got the biggest charge out of me, as

I got into one of my silly moods and couldn't stop laughing. The rest of the afternoon we looked at the "Punch" magazine, similar to the "New Yorker," which is published in England. Some of the cartoons were darling. I read all the artists and underlined all the words I didn't understand so Brian could explain them to me. One phrase the English used often in this magazine, "you rotten jerk," seemed a bit harsh. I used to say "can" harshly, especially with a nasal sound, which Brian, with his good Oxford diction, says now. The rest of the English people started to pick up my phrases.

When I came home from my appendix operation in Singapore, Brian and I dated quite a bit. Also, he spoiled me by giving me something all the time. He sent to Singapore for some Elizabeth Arden lipstick and when it arrived, I was in Singapore, so he gave it to me when I got back home. I didn't tell him that I had gotten two new tubes while I was away. Last night he presented me with an ivory pin with a Chinese scene and characters on it.

One Friday, one of Brian's bosses from London arrived in Sibu unexpectedly. I just had a dress made of pea green nylon trimmed in black velvet, sleeveless, low in front and back with a three-tiered skirt to wear to our dinner together. From what Brian told me about his meeting, his boss asked him how he liked the area. Brian had hopes of going to British Columbia on his next term. Well, the boss convinced him to stay in Sibu, and I could put two and two together and believed it included me.

Sunday morning, when Brian walked into his office to drive the head boss to the airport to catch his plane to Singapore, he asked Brian if I was going to see him off. He was only in Sibu a day and a half, but he had learned a great deal about Brian's private life. He was a young chap who had inherited the company—a great sports car racer in all the Grand Prix on the Continent and in England.

Brian's birthday, October 23, was on a Saturday, so I planned a menu of hamburgers, rolls, baked potatoes, tomatoes, and a coconut birthday cake to take to a picnic at the airport.

One evening Brian invited a few friends to a "before dinner drinks" party, which was supposed to last 1½ hours, but we didn't leave until 9 p.m. Although Brian and I hadn't eaten dinner, we decided to attend the late show and then eat. By the time the movie was over, it was 11 p.m., so we went to "Li Ling" to cook dinner. I didn't get to bed until 1 a.m. Brian didn't ride his motorcycle, so the poor dear had to walk home about 1½ miles. If the tide was in, he would have had to roll up his pants and walk barefoot because it was below sea level where he lived. I was probably asleep by the time he reached home, for I was exhausted even before I went out at 7 p.m.

One Tuesday afternoon, Brian and I spent three hours watering his boss's flowers and vegetables, as he and his wife had left on a six-week leave visiting Rome and London. Afterwards we ate dinner, dashed to the club and saw a movie. Wednesday evening was usually prayer meeting, and on one of those evenings Judy, Ellen and I went to see the movie "The Cruel Sea." It was typically English, the way they ate and the "jolly" phrases they said. After it was over at 9:15 p.m., we decided to see another movie, "Salome," which was the only night I could see it, as Brian and I had been invited to one of the bachelor's dinner parties the next day. When I received a letter that one of my friends had married, I wished in a way that I was married. But then I thought of the wonderful times I was having seeing the world. However, Mrs. Brian Casidy didn't sound bad. If I hadn't had two more years of work facing me, I would have given in and married someone, but Brian knew the obligations I faced. I was afraid he wouldn't come back to Sibu. He probably would go back to London, work in the main office and become a director or something big.

Marge Hooper, the missionary who was stationed in Ipoh and came with Ellen and me on the "MS Tabinta," stayed in Sibu for a three-week vacation. She met the Sibu bachelors: Brian, Tony, Seth, and Ian, and we had a great party time! Judy said she could hear Tony's laughter at her home across the Malay cemetery. We had a nice time. Seth was nice to Marge, and he saw her again at the Europeans farewell party for the Borneo Company manager, who was going on leave. The next night, we were invited to the resident physician and wife's home. Then we left with them on Sunday morning to go upriver to show Marge much of Sarawak.

On May 17, 1954, I wrote a letter to my college suitemate, Joyce Lawson, hoping it would reach her before Carol Ann arrived to spend the weekend with her. I wrote saying, "I hope you two don't sit up all night talking like I do when I visit friends. Two weekends ago, Tony, Brian, and I went to Sarikei to spend the night with Tony's girl, Irma. She and I went to bed around 11 p.m. talking until 2 a.m. The fellows did likewise, but they didn't laugh and giggle like we did. On Sunday, we got up early to go swimming in the South China Sea taking Brian's company 30' inboard speed boat. We couldn't have picked a better weekend, as the surf was wonderful in which to swim. The only trouble is that we had to watch out for jelly fish swimming since Brian had been stung by one. I spent some time picking up seashells along the shore which looked different from the ones I had picked up in Florida. Coming back, the tide coming in had enormous waves while the wind blew, almost sinking our boat. I'm glad I kept my bathing suit on, as we were getting soaking wet. It was the only sensible thing I did all weekend. By the time we got back to Sibu on Sunday evening, we were exhausted. I fed Brian and Tony a light supper and bid them goodnight and went to bed.

One weekend Brian went down river on a job, so Tony was left in Sibu. Ted, who ran a timber mill, came to Sibu for a change of scenery, so Tony and he called on me for a short visit. Saturday afternoon they took Ellen and me upriver to visit some Norwegian people, after which, we went dancing at the Island Club. Later in the evening, we received an invitation to dinner from the leading Chinese businessman of Sibu. His purpose for inviting us was to see if I would teach him to play the piano. He had a delicious Chinese dinner—whole chicken in a broth which included the chicken head and feet, shark fin soup, and whole fish with the head and tail cut up in small bits, so it was easy to eat with chopsticks.

On Sunday, Brian and I went swimming at the airport, played with naked little Chinese boys throwing mud and sand balls at each other. In the evening, we saw the movie, "The Thief" with Ray Milland. There was no dialogue, and it was a very intense picture. It was such fun to see the sights in Washington, New York and do a tour of the Empire State Building with Brian.

During the last week of school, 230 men of the British Navy prepared for active duty sailed into Sibu. Every night someone was giving a party. Friday night, the Island Club threw a big party, and I had so much fun, the only single girl, for Ellen was scared to go. Tony escorted me, and I didn't get home until 1:30 a.m. I ate curry puffs all night. I can't wait to get home to cook some of this wonderful food. Sunday morning at 7 a.m., we went to the airport to watch the English Sibu men vs. the Navy play cricket.

Monday evening, we watched Rugby. Brian came back that day from his business trip and played an excellent game. That evening, the Resident invited me to a party attended by the officers. I arrived home at 2 a.m. In my letter to Carol Ann, I wrote, "Did you ever think you would hear all this activity from me, especially a missionary stuck out here in Borneo?"

When the Island Club had a Halloween Party, it was different from any that I had ever experienced. An hour before attending it, I was told that the women would be wearing long formal dresses to keep the mosquitoes from biting their legs, so there would be no dunking for apples. I suggested some games to play and decorations to use, for the English didn't celebrate Halloween. They attempted to have hot dogs, but some of the women wanted to use pork sausage, for they didn't know that some people didn't eat pork. I insisted that we buy hot dogs which came in tins in Borneo. I saved Ellen, Brian, and myself some good American hot dogs, but I ruined mine by using too much mustard. It had been prepared with dry mustard instead of regular mustard. It was so hot that tears flowed from Ellen's and my eyes.

In December 1954, I had a wonderful trip with Brian up the Rejang and Melinau Rivers in the Hose Mountains to visit the Dayak longhouse of Penghulu Sibat, whose daughter was one of my students. We left Sibu in a slow-moving Chinese boat to travel upriver to Kapit, which took the whole day, so we stayed with missionary teachers overnight. The next day we hired a longboat, a driver, and a lookout, who sat up front and directed the driver around the rocks and rapids. In some areas, we had to carry the boat, arriving at Penghulu Sibat's longhouse in the early afternoon. This trip gave me a different impression of Borneo for Kapit was beautiful in comparison to Sibu. It was located on the south bank of the Rejang River noted for its longhouses and timber camps.

Thanksgiving Dinner

Chapter 7

The Engagement

Trying to carry on a courtship with three sixty-year-old spinsters watching over us was difficult and not acceptable to them. Consequently, we tried to stay out of their way as much as we could and travel around the limited mileage of roads on Brian's motorbike or the Land Rover if it was available. We also spent time at the bomb crater swimming pool at the airport, going to the movies, or out to dinner. The three ladies were eventually won over, and they arranged the engagement party on my birthday. God bless them.

On January 4, 1955, the date of my 24th birthday, my engagement to Brian Casidy of London, England was announced at a party organized by the three ladies who lived with me at "Li Ling." My mother, Mildred Wingert, published my engagement in the Elmira Gazette newspaper on January 14, 1955:

"Miss Katherine M. Wingert, daughter of Mrs. Laban Wingert of 517 W. Church St, and the late Mr. Wingert, and Brian Casidy of London, England, made known their engagement recently at a party at the home of the Rev. and Mrs. Douglas Coole in Sibu, Sarawak. Miss Wingert is a graduate of local schools and Keuka College. She is a missionary teacher in the Methodist Mission School in Sibu. Her fiancé graduated from Eltham College and is employed by Montague L. Meyer, Sarawak timber exporters. The wedding will be solemnized in Sibu in September."

On January 13, 1955, Carol Ann called Joyce Lawson telling her that my engagement was to be announced in the Elmira paper. This is what Joyce wrote to me on that date.

"After bolting down my dinner, I dashed upstairs, got my typewriter out, and am now trying very hard to tell you how very happy I am for both Brian and you. I can well remember promising you that I would send a cable if and when I became engaged or married while you were away, and here we are with the table completely turned. Just wish I had a recording of Carol's conversation. She was bubbling and laughing like always and there was a bit of screaming, too. Said she would be sure to send me a paper. Also reported that this young man will be around this area in April, so Miss Patterson and I have appointed us a committee of two to pass opinion. Golly, I can hardly wait to meet him! No wonder I haven't heard from you in just ages!"

The big test for both of us was when Brian went on home leave for four months, which began on April 12, 1955. Because the company wanted him to go via Vancouver to study forest practices there, and because he would take the opportunity to visit my mother in Elmira, New York, who was planning a reception on June 5 for Brian to meet my family and friends to which I had mailed slides of our engagement party, he would be away longer than the four months. Also, he would visit Carol Ann at Keuka College and Marie McGrath, a Pan American flight attendant and college friend, in New York City before flying back to London. As it stood now, Brian might not be back in Sibu until late August. Since we met in March 1954, we had not been apart from each other for longer than two weeks. Brian was terrified that I might find someone else while he was away, although I told him that would not happen. I could see that he was worried.

When Brian left on April 12, he wrote to me at least once every two days and, after the first month, brought up the subject again of me finding someone else. He repeated his concern in many letters thereafter, but he must have realized later that nothing terrible would happen because I wrote to him every second day also. His letters continued to come from Hong Kong, Japan, Vancouver, and on the train to Philadelphia. Then many letters from Elmira, New York City, and London, England. They continued with Brian's holiday to Paris and Copenhagen. Brian was seeing the world while I was stuck in Sibu.

I wished I could have gone with him, but I kept telling myself that I wanted to be a missionary, so I must stick to my three-year contract. I did, however, take a short holiday to Singapore and Malaysia with Judy Tan, a fellow teacher and one of the bridesmaids to be. There were many times when I felt lost and alone, but our friends in Sibu invited me to lunches, dinners, and other social events, so it could have been worse. Also, I had my work to keep me occupied.

Shortly after Brian arrived in London, he went into the office and arranged for the return trip earlier than planned on August 4. We arranged for a phone call to be made to me while

I was in Singapore. These were the days when you had to book the call a day in advance and the reception was usually poor. Consequently, it was less than perfect, but at least we heard each other's voices after two months apart.

Captain Bloem (aged about 55) was master of the ship San Fernando on which Brian had often worked as an agent. When hearing that Clara French from the Methodist Mission Board was trying to torpedo my marriage to Brian, he said, "When two normal people are in love, everything else is of secondary importance and the love of the two people will continue and grow and nothing outside can change it." He said to Brian when he heard that he was leaving me behind for four months or more in Sibu, "Brian, you are an idiot. If I were 30 years or even 25 years younger, you would lose her." His prediction did not materialize, Brian arrived back early, and we started to finalize plans for the wedding and reception.

The Methodist Mission staff, led by my three old lady housemates, hosted a wedding shower for me. What a change of heart from a year earlier. I felt that Carol Ann would really like Brian. When I wrote her on May 21, 1955, I said "By this time, you should have met Brian. From what I have heard from him, he has lost weight, so maybe he won't look in person like his pictures. Anyway, I think he is tops and you would like him."

In my letter on June 16, 1955, to Carol Ann, I told her that when Brian was in New York City, he visited with my boss, Dr. French, and found out that I would only need to pay $50 for not completing my three-year contract once I was married. Brian wrote me that he was very much impressed with Carol Ann and Keuka.

After I told him about some of the funny things we did, he could now visualize them. I wished that Carol Ann could take a trip out here. We could have so much fun. I was so excited when I received my letter from Carol Ann, I could hardly open it correctly to find her reaction to Brian, which I learned was very positive. She really liked him, and she was so happy for both of us. "If I ever get back to see you, I'll probably sit up all night talking to you. I hope Brian will understand. Really, Carol, you don't know how I'm looking forward to coming home for Christmas in 1957."

Finally, I wrote my friend, Bill in Elmira, NY, who was serious about marrying me. I had delayed writing him for three weeks to tell him that there wasn't any hope for us to be married. I didn't know what type of person he would turn out to be, one who would never marry or would marry at the first opportunity.

Brian returned to Sibu from his leave on August 4, 1955.

Aerial View of Sibu, 1954

Dayak warriors

Sibu floods, 1955

Dayak boy fishing

Ellen and Dottie at graduation from Hoover Memorial School

Ellen, Dottie, and Judy

Dayak lady in her finery, silver belt and coins

Christmas Pageant
Dottie on left and Judy on right

School children with Dottie and Ellen

Tuck Wai, Ellen, and Dottie

Ellen, Brian, and Dottie in 1954

Sibu Police Officer #179

Brian Casidy

Dottie and Gibbon

Brian and Dottie in 1954

Mrs. Laban W. Wingert

announces the marriage of her daughter

Katherine

to

Mr. Brian Edwin Casidy

on Saturday, the twenty-fourth of September

Nineteen hundred and fifty-five

Sibu, Sarawak

Laban, Mildred, and Randall Wingert

Keuka friends

Photograph by Bill Banaszewski,
Finger Lakes Images Publishers

Dottie, Carol Ann, and Joyce

Carol Ann, Dottie, Joyce, and Isy
Keuka Reunion

Carol Ann and Dottie

Carol Ann and Dottie in Jacksonville, Florida

Carol Ann and Brian

Shanghai

Brian and Dottie in Jacksonville, Florida

Brian, Sydney, and Dottie

Carol Ann, Ernest Jernigan, and Dottie in Ocala, Florida

Chapter 8

September 24, 1955 – The Wedding

Since Brian and I had made known our engagement on January 4, 1955, we spent the rest of January, February, and March making plans for our wedding, where and what type.

When I knew I was planning to be married, I wrote to the regional office in Singapore to tell them of my plans. I asked for their blessings and permission to continue teaching after the honeymoon.

European weddings hardly ever happened in Sibu, and European church weddings almost never happened, so this venture of ours will be something to remember for all concerned. Since Brian was going on leave for four months from April 12 to the end of August, we chose September 24 to be our wedding date. When he visited my mother in the States, they could print the wedding announcements.

The four-month separation was hard, because we had practically been on each other's doorsteps for months. We ate out together, went to movies together, took walks, and motorbike rides together. I knew from Brian's letters that he was scared that I might change my mind about the engagement while he was away. He mentioned this fear in many letters to me and, although I told him it would not happen, he continued to worry.

After Brian left, I had plenty of time to dream about the wedding. When I went to Singapore for my summer vacation, my wedding dress materialized into a full-length nylon, tulle dress with a small train of lovely old lace given to me by Mrs. Petrie of Elmira. The top part of the dress was also made from old lace with short sleeves forming a long point to the elbows. The skirt was lovely and full, making a fluffy affect for the hot weather of tropical Sarawak.

Judy Tan and Ellen Atkinson's bridesmaid dresses were made by a Chinese lady in Sibu, who copied the style from a magazine—a V-neck, a full four-gore skirt, and hidden sleeves. The outer dress was made from a thin nylon material and the slip from taffeta in matching colors: Judy wearing lilac and Ellen wearing powder blue.

After a four-month leave, Brian came back early to help with the rest of the wedding plans. The first major activity was to mail the invitations to the wedding and reception. We didn't want a large reception, but it was extremely difficult to limit the invitations. The Resident, Dennis White, who would give me away, graciously offered his home for the reception. Douglas Coole, principal of the Methodist School in Sibu, was to officiate at the wedding, but about six weeks before the wedding, he took ill with yellow jaundice.

We were hoping he would be on his feet by the time of the wedding. It so happened that this wedding was Doug's liberation from confinement, allowing him to go into public places to associate with friends again. Martha McCutcheon and Polly Coole were asked to decorate the Masland Memorial Methodist Church with instructions not to decorate, as the Chinese do, with elaborate decorations of crepe in bright reds, oranges, greens, and blues and millions of artificial flowers.

On Friday afternoon, the school children polished the church furniture and altar, which had never been polished before in its entire existence. Since the church was one building, there wasn't a room for the bride and groom to sign the official register. This was solved by making a semi-private corner with a screen to the right of the altar where two bridesmaids, usher, best man, father, minister, bride and groom could squeeze in while Mrs. Ian Proud sung "Where Thou Goeth" from the story of Ruth. By the time we signed the register, Phyllis would be finished singing, and we could walk out of the church with big, beaming smiles, waiting for the photographer to take some unbelievable pictures.

Another problem—Sibu had no catering services. The nearest catering services were in Singapore, but strikes were going on there, so what kinds of food could we serve at the reception? The wedding cake was being made by a Malay woman, who had taken special cake decorating training in Singapore. I bought her cake mixes and advised her to make a three-tiered cake on pillars, using only white icing and no coloring because Malays loved to use coloring. We found a man to make curry puffs. My Girl Guides made over a hundred, open faced, colored cream cheese and egg salad sandwiches. Connie Smith, the best man's wife, filled pastry cups with melted cheese early Saturday morning. The night before the wedding, I made a special point to see the boys, who were serving drinks and food at the reception, to be sure they were making the punch.

During the week of the wedding, there were a million things to do but that was difficult, as many things could not be done until the day of the wedding. I had school on Friday morning and Brian had his job, so the afternoon was spent packing for our honeymoon, seeing to last minute details at the church, the residency, performing the rehearsal and preparing the rehearsal dinner.

Late Friday afternoon, the cake was brought to the residency where we discovered no safe place to put it, for there were four dogs that lived there, thousands of ants dying to taste it, and rats and cockroaches loving to eat it before the cake was cut. It rested on a table in the middle of the ground floor sitting room with its legs standing in saucers of water with a chemical on top to keep the rats and cockroaches away. All night long, I thought of the wedding cake being eaten, a pleasant thing to be thinking about the night before the wedding.

Friday evening, after the rehearsal, everyone involved in the wedding were at "Li Ling" helping to prepare the dinner. Martha Graf, Palmie, and Martha McCutcheon did a lovely job making the house look wonderful. Judy and Ellen brought all they needed to spend the night with us, and they pitched in to help with the dinner. I was late getting home and Brian was even later. Halfway through dinner, the lady mission folk disappeared and reappeared in outrageous clothing representing a wedding party.

Palmie was the blushing bride, Martha Graf the groom, McCutcheon the preacher, Madeline and Polly, the matron of honor and best man respectively, and Ellen played the villain. They all pranced down the stairs in a jazzy sort of way and proceeded to carry on a wedding in a similar fashion. Martha Graf was really swinging it. At first, the Resident, sitting prim and proper, didn't know what to make of it. Finally, he couldn't refrain from laughing because everyone was busting their sides with laughter. Mike Jarvis, usher, Pete Smith, the best man, and Ian Proud couldn't believe their eyes.

The funniest thing about the whole skit was when the villain kicked the preacher in the pulpit, and Ellen didn't crack a smile. All in all, the dinner party was quite a success with 18 people present: the bride to be, the groom to be, Judy, Ellen, Martha Graf, Martha McCutcheon, Annie Pittman, Emma Palm, Madeline and Louis Dennis, Ian and Phyllis Proud, Mike Jarvis, Peter and Connie Smith, the Resident Dennis White, and Polly and Doug Coole.

The wedding morning was planned to the last minute. Three taxis were ordered for the morning, one at 8 a.m. to take the usher to the church, another to fetch the best man and drive to pick up Brian to see that he was properly dressed and at the church at 8:30 a.m., and the third to take the bridesmaids to the church. The Resident arrived in his car, a Sunbeam Talbot, and took me to the church. We were out of the church, photographs taken and to the residency for the reception right on schedule, because at 11 a.m. we had to be at the airport to fly the first hop of our honeymoon to Hong Kong.

About 55 guests, mostly from Sibu, were at the reception with a few friends who flew in from Kuching. Lynn Lawrence and Connie Smith brought the carnation bouquets for me and the bridesmaids, which were ordered in Kuching but made in Singapore. Throughout the reception, little Rosalie Dennis was in her glory, holding onto my dress.

When Brian and I posed to have our pictures taken, we laughed so hard while cutting the cake, because it was so hard, we couldn't get our knife through it. The cake was lovely, but little was eaten, so Ellen collected all the food, drink, and cake and gave it to the hostel girls.

When we drove off to the airport, four-gallon size kerosene tins were tied to the back of our car and what a noise they made! The local people were really amused with such horse play. On our suitcases, Ian and a few other men wrote "Almost Married" and "In Sibu Too." The wives and Ellen had put tons of rice on us, inside us and confetti in our suitcases. Brian, with his arms and legs dangling, was carried to the plane by the gallant men of Sibu. The captain of the plane was warned in Singapore that a newly married couple was getting on in Sibu, getting off in Labuan, and to make their trip pleasant. A white ribbon was tied to the wing of the plane. The captain dipped the plane over Sibu and to the crowd gathered below and invited us into his small compartment. We were off to Hong Kong, leaving people to celebrate without us.

After the wedding, Ellen Atkinson, one of the bridesmaids, wrote the following account of the activities to our mothers. She wanted them to know how well everything went.

"The past week has been hectic, and all of us have been run ragged. There were always so many things that couldn't be done until the last minute, and then you wonder when you'll find time to get them all done before the crucial moment. Well, anyway, we did get everything finished, and the whole thing went off as scheduled...in fact, a few minutes ahead of schedule.

Thursday afternoon was spent making the sandwiches, etc. and getting all lined up for the reception. That night Brian was attending a stag party, bidding "farewell" to all the bachelors. A group of us went to the movies. I got to bed early that night. Friday, we ran around the whole day. The dresses had to be pressed, the church decorated, the place of the reception arranged, packing to be done, etc.

The rehearsal was at 6 p.m. and all the wedding party showed up dressed ready for the dinner, which followed except the bride and groom, who were both about as tacky looking as I've seen them, but then no one minded. They had just come from the residency taking care of last minute things.

Following the dinner, the women of the mission group put on a skit—a takeoff on the wedding, and it was a scream. If you only knew the ones who took part, you could appreciate it much better. They will no doubt write you all about it, so I won't go into detail here. To say the least though, everyone was doubled over with laughter— more at the costumes than anything else.

After the dinner, we still had things to take to the residency, so we hurried around doing that. We managed, however, to get to bed before midnight. None of us slept much though, due to all the excitement. I was up before 6 a.m. the next morning, cutting flowers to be placed on Judy's and my hat. Then I had to take the remainder of the things down to the residency. We all got dressed on time, the taxis, etc. arrived on schedule, and we reached the church only about 2 or 3 minutes late. The ceremony went very well, but the preacher was the most nervous. We wondered for a moment if he was going to drop his book.

The church was decorated nicely with green palms and ferns and looked the best I've ever seen it. Oh, we did it up in style, even had an aisle cloth. The weather treated us nicely. It was a bit cloudy and looked as if it might rain, with except for a few sprinkles at the reception, it was clear and not too hot. The reception was lovely and the cake, baked by a Malay, couldn't have been more beautiful if it had been made in New York or London. I'm sending a small piece off to each of you, just for the fun of it.

Everyone was dressed fit to kill. I told Dottie, the way things turned out and everyone made such a fuss over this wedding, I think it's the biggest occasion in Sibu since the Coronation of Queen Elizabeth. All the ladies had new dresses, stockings, hats, and many of them even wore girdles, which was an unheard thing in Sibu. Dot and I both had ours on for the first time since we got off the boat in Penang two years ago.

Most of the people went to the airport to see them off. When the time came to get on the plane, the fellows literally carried Brian to the plane. After the takeoff, the pilot circled the airfield, and made a low swoop, so we all waved them farewell. So, those are the highlights of the wedding. You can both be very proud of them. They are most happy, and I think, couldn't be better suited for each other. As far as I'm concerned, Dot couldn't have found a better man anywhere, and Brian got one of the sweetest girls I've ever known. I am sure they both are extremely happy. Oh, yes, both of your telegrams, along with many others, arrived at the residency about midway through the reception. They were read and very much appreciated.

Dot made a lovely bride. Her gown was beautiful. Having met Brian, I know you feel as I do, that he's one of the grandest guys I've known. Dot's a lucky girl."

Mr. and Mrs. Brian Casidy
September 24, 1955

Chapter 9

The Honeymoon

After the wedding ceremony at 11:30 a.m., Brian and I flew to Labuan Island off the Northwest Coast of Sarawak on a DC3, where we spent the night. The following day, we took a Quantas Airways DC4 to Hong Kong. This flight originated in Sydney, then Darwin, then Labuan where we stayed overnight on September 24. We stayed the first night of our married life in a government rest house, as there were no good hotels in Labuan. We explored the island before dark and saw the allied war cemetery where some people's deaths happened after the war had officially ended because the local Japanese weren't told about the surrender. The island also had some lovely beaches. Early on September 25, we left on Qantas for a non-stop flight to Hong Kong. There was a typhoon warning for Hong Kong, but the pilot decided to try it. It was an extremely bumpy end to the flight and a scary landing. We thought, "Is our life going to end before the honeymoon?" Only two flights landed that day.

In Hong Kong, Brian and I stayed at the Repulse Bay Hotel, a lovely colonial type building on Repulse Bay around the back of Hong Kong Island. A gorgeous spot whose beach was packed on weekends but almost empty during the week.

In Sibu, Brian's company was agents for a Hong Kong shipping company, Manners Navigation, owned by a Portuguese family called de la Sala. They regularly came into the river's anchorage in Sarawak and loaded a whole ship load of logs, which they took to Hong Kong for processing. Well, the de la Sala family and senior executives really did us proud. They took us out for lunches, dinner, special trips, etc. It was fantastic. They even loaned us a car and driver for the day. At the suggestion of the Manners Company, we took a ferry trip to Macau where another Manners person, Mr. Monteiro, met the ferry, drove us to a small hotel and showed us around the Portuguese Colony. Then, we went back to Hong Kong for more swimming, dinner courtesy of Manners Navigation and shopping. We still have a rosewood coffee table and nest of tables that we bought while we were there in 1955.

The plane stopped overnight in Manila on our return to Sibu; Marie McGrath, a Keuka College colleague and Pan American Airline flight attendant, met us. Marie said it was more than a coincidental 5,000 to 1 shot when she thought of all the variables, of how Brian and I were only in Manila overnight and that she was there too at the same hotel, for her very first time, of how she was nearly diverted to Tokyo, and our planes being five hours late. (If we had been two hours later, she would have missed us completely.) When Marie thought of all these possible obstacles, she was convinced providence was smiling upon us in that remote, exotic part of the world. What a reunion we had as Marie and I hadn't seen each other since graduation from Keuka. Knowing Brian already, Marie didn't seem like an intruder waking us at 4:30 a.m. On our honeymoon, Brian had two girls on his bed, chatting away on our reunion. Marie said, "He was certainly a peach to put up with all that women talk." It was quite an exciting event.

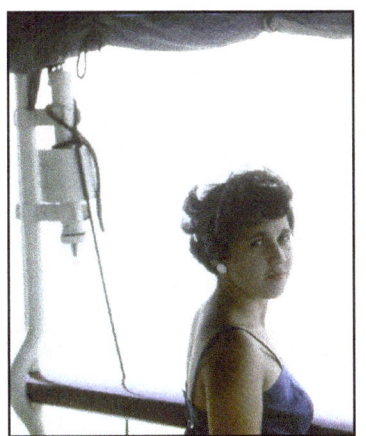

Dottie on ferry from Hong Kong to Macau

Dottie and Brian in Macau in 1955

Chapter 10

Married Life in Sibu

After the wonderful honeymoon in Hong Kong and Macau, Brian, and I returned to Sibu in October 1955 where we lived in a rented house. Brian continued working for Montague L. Meyer Ltd., and I resumed teaching at the Methodist Mission Primary School.

Married life was idyllic. On Sundays, we prepared curry "tiffins" (lunches) often and on various weekends many of the bachelors, other young couples, and two single nurses were invited. Although the house was far from a mansion, it was, however, much better than where Brian had lived previously, but not as luxurious as my old house "Li Ling." We did have lights, sewage and running water, although sometimes there were glitches with the water purification plant. Brian was a dear, as I just mentioned that I wished I had a washing machine, and he purchased one for me. If I was going to wash most of my own laundry, I didn't want to scrub dirty clothes on a rack all afternoon like the Chinese workers do so they don't last long. Wearing clothes in the tropics was different from home where I could wear a cotton dress for two or three days, but in Sibu they got smelly after four to six hours. We had to have lots of clothes here. I liked to wear skirts and blouses in the mornings when it was cooler because they were warmer, and in the afternoon and evening, dresses were cooler.

I really enjoyed teaching, and I had been appointed Dean of the Primary School. It seemed as though life could not get any better. Some of our friends had moved away, but there was a core of people who we had known for two or three years and because Sibu did not offer very much else, their friendships were important. Also, Brian and I no longer had to carry on a courtship under the watchful eyes of three 60-year-old spinsters.

Carol Ann didn't hear from me until New Year's 1956—the Chinese New Year when Brian and I we were in full swing with all the celebrating and feasting at a formal dinner party with the Sibu Europeans at the Island Club where I wore my red dress, white satin shoes, and Brian's wedding gift of magnolias set in silver. We also attended a dinner dance at the Chinese Club where I knew we wouldn't be able to hear anyone talk for the noise of the firecrackers.

My two-day vacation from teaching went all too fast, and the opening of school was terrible, as we had to turn away many children for whom we had no room. Our classes were so large with 42 to 55 students.

One week Brian and I went into the jungle to dig up some grown orchids, so he could take them down river to a sea captain who raised flowers on board ship outside his room. The captain sent back some rich Java soil and stamps. It was amazing what we traded for in Sibu. Brian and I collected some queer things.

In my garden, I planted over 100 tomato plants, 50 papaya trees, six pineapple plants, three different kinds of orchids, and an assortment of flowers. I wished that Carol Ann could have been in Sibu to enjoy my surroundings and see where I lived. On February 9, 1956, I wrote her that I had received her wedding gift, a thermos container, that I used for hot soups. It was extremely useful as I did most of my cooking on one electric hot plate.

Brian went down river quite often, supervising the loading of timber on the ships from Hong Kong. One time he took my Zenith radio, hoping that the ship's radio operator could repair it, but he said that the Zenith dealer in Hong Kong would have to fix it. This radio gave me so much trouble all the time that I had it.

When I wrote to Carol Ann on March 10, 1956, I asked her, "Are there any signs of spring around Keuka? I wondered if Mrs. Loomis, one of my birding friends from Keuka days, would be watching for the Red Wing Blackbirds and Pipets going North. My mother had written that geese had been seen near Bath. I wrote that I enjoyed watching the tiny black sparrows, the beautiful bitsy red birds and the familiar Malayan black and white robins build their nests. I could even see the chickens laying eggs under our house, so the poor people who had fed them wouldn't make any money.

Brian received his alumni news one day and found an old boy by the name of Colin Barrow, who went to Eltham College about the same time as he, had received a three year

Fulbright Grant at the University of Florida, where he was teaching part-time while working on a degree. Since Carol Ann was a graduate student there, I wrote to her saying, "If you ever run into him, say we hope to see him and his wife in Florida."

When Brian went down river for four days, I was so scared to be in the house alone one night, as a rat bit my thumb while I was in my bed. I finally got enough courage to turn on the desk lamp to see if he had gone. The next night Brian was home and caught the rat, chopped it into bits and burned it. The night before that rat had stolen two potatoes that I was going to fry for my dinner. I had gone into the living room to turn on my radio and when I came back, they were gone. For two days, we had no water. The watermain had broken, so Brian and I took baths at the airport's bomb crater where we swam in very warm water. I would rather swim and bathe in that pool than go to the dirty Rejang River where everyone went.

We had some excitement in Sibu when the boss from Australia for whom Brian might work, Clara French and Tracey Jones from the New York Methodist Mission Office, two people from America who wanted to make movies of mission work, and the Governor of Sarawak all arrived about the same time.

In March of 1956, Brian's company mentioned that the number two man in their Singapore office, who worked for a sister company called Malayan Timber and Trading (MTT), was going on leave in May, and they would like Brian to take over his job. Brian and I talked this over, and we agreed that it would be a good idea, but I would stay in Sibu until the end of the school year in early to mid-June.

We needed to begin packing our belongings and selling those items that were duplicates or might break in traveling. We had boxes made for our furniture, and I had given my religious education books to the Bible School Library and my storybooks to the mission school.

I was looking forward to a bit of living in Singapore. One of the bachelors in Sibu had offered us his car to keep the battery running while we were in Singapore, so I was looking forward to traveling around the city. When Brian was gone down river again for five days, I was getting things organized for the Girl Guide Commissioner of Borneo, who was arriving that same week. Also, I was giving finals which meant grading papers and marking grades on the students' report cards.

It was May 4, 1956, when I wrote to Carol Ann, "How does it feel to be working in President Blyley's office? With the closing of the college around the corner, May Day and all, I bet it is buzzing. I imagine spring is delightful with sunbathing starting soon after such a cold, snowy winter. Brian always remembers the girls sunbathing on the lawn, wishing he and Ran could have had a better view. When we get back to Keuka this summer, where there are so many things to do and see, I must drive Brian on the road around the Bluff which he missed last time. I hope we can get together with you in August or September.

Just over a year ago, Brian was gone on his world tour. Now a year later, he's left again, not on a world tour but to Singapore. He was off on Monday's plane, and I'm staying behind until June 14 when I fly to Singapore. School closes the next day. Brian will fly in on June 15, so after five weeks we will be together. Finally, step by step, we are leaving Sibu."

We had been attempting to pack, but there had been something every night prior to Brian's departure on Monday. I hoped we would be serious about packing, as I couldn't pack heavy furniture or seal it against weather and thieving. I was 3 to 4 months pregnant, and I did not want to lift anything heavy. I was taking the luggage to Singapore with me, but we would not use any of it while we were there. At this time, I thought we would be in Singapore until late October, and then I hoped we would be on leave and home for the holidays, after which we would go to Australia as planned.

It all seemed like a dream. I was already imaging the things I would be doing in Singapore as a lady of leisure, no teaching. Brian would be looking for a place for us to rent when he was transferred to Singapore in May. My greatest joy would be having a car to drive. Since we expected to be there six months, I planned to visit my friends in the Federation of Malaya. Brian hadn't been off Singapore Island, so there would be a million things to do and see. By the time I reached the United States, my friends would see me back in my normal state, not wild and woolly like I was in Sarawak. I hoped these plans would materialize when it was time to see Carol Ann in December or January in Florida.

Brian returned to Sibu on a Sunday, but was off on a business trip, visiting some nearby sawmills. So, I, with the help of clerks in the office, worked Tuesday and Wednesday evenings packing fourteen wooden boxes. I sent three small boxes of Sarawak arts and crafts home, thinking Brian and I might open a shop in my mother's garage, selling Borneo and Malayan handiworks to help finance some of our leave in the United States.

I couldn't wait to see Carol Ann this winter in Florida and spend some time reminiscing. It sounded like we would be scattered over the world at that time. I was hoping Joyce could take her vacation then, so we could be together in Florida.

I had messed things up because a wee one would be arriving in late October or early November and no one would take an expectant mother on a plane, so we thought we would wait in Singapore and then go home in January with a little girl (ha!). By that time, I would be back in shape to wear my long and very tight Chinese dress. I was hoping that Joyce gave Marie our address, so when she flew through to Singapore, she would be able to see us, and I could show her the sights. I let Elsie know when I was in town.

And so, the long business of saying goodbye to Sarawak and the friends that we had made there was to begin. Sarawak, a country that neither Brian nor I had even heard about five years earlier, had become a very special place—a place where we had met, courted, gotten engaged, married, and conceived our first child, Mark.

Goodbyes were given to friends, Chinese, Malays, Ibans, British, Dutch, and Australians, with whom we had enjoyed good times for over three years. Many of these people we would never see again. Some of them, however, would be transferred to Singapore, where old memories would be rekindled.

As the years went by, we met Brian's boss, Tim Dix, again in England, after his retirement from working in Southeast Asia. Brian would also meet the usher from our wedding, Mike Jarvis, on a business trip to Bangkok 25 years later. Another friend, David Brennan, met us in Singapore many years later.

On a trip to Australia in 1991, we would spend four days with one of our bridesmaids, Judy Tan Geck Kee in Cairns, Australia. She had emigrated, settled in subtropical Cairns, married a Frenchman, who had unfortunately died from cancer before our visit. The other bridesmaid, Ellen Atkinson, had returned to the United States after many more years in Sarawak. We met her in Torrance, California.

Other friends from Sarawak, although never seen face to face again, kept in touch for many years. All are wonderful memories that we would remember forever. We were two young people from different parts of the world, meeting in Sibu, Sarawak, and then spending a lifetime together.

Chapter II

Singapore, Malaysia

In May 1956, Brian was transferred to Singapore, and I stayed in Sibu to continue teaching until late in my pregnancy in order to fulfil my three-year contract, which I almost did.

Brian was very busy as soon as he moved to Singapore. He had to learn the job of the fellow who was going on home leave, make out the residency applications and work permits and look for some place for us to live when I arrived in June. He was extremely lucky, because when talking to an old friend from Sibu, Lionel Storrs, he was told that a friend in his company was going on home leave for six months and wanted to rent his house. However, it would have to be to someone that he knew and trusted or someone that Lionel knew. Brian and I had been friends with Lionel and his wife Thelma in Sibu, and that was good enough. Brian and his company were able to finalize a deal where he and I rented the house with two servants, two dogs, and a small car. It belonged to a couple who had lived in Singapore for 25 years. It was located about four miles from the city and near a swimming pool and hotel. What an incredible change from Sibu! The house was a pre-war bungalow with two bedrooms (one air-conditioned), dressing room, spacious living and dining rooms, and a lovely patio where we held barbecues on a regular basis.

Although I was four to five months pregnant, I enjoyed my exciting new life, and I was losing instead of gaining weight. The doctor, a charming man with an unfortunate name, Dr. Coffin, checked me out thoroughly and said that I was "fit as a fiddle" and that he was not concerned about the weight loss. His confidence in my health was a relief. We went swimming most weekends at either Changi Beach or Pasir Ris. On many Saturday evenings, we had barbecues at the house. The meat was courtesy of the absent homeowner, who was in the shipping business and had a standing order for Australian steaks every two weeks arriving frozen on one of his ships. I reveled in the Singapore style of life and continued to be extremely fit despite the baby's arrival getting closer. Brian said my energy and enthusiasm was very catching. In my July 14, 1956 letter to Carol Ann, I wrote:

"Elsie Gan came to see us last Sunday evening. It was the first time Brian had seen her; he kept calling her Vivian. Bit by bit, he would meet all the Class of '53. Beginning this weekend, she'll be on a two week vacation, so I told her to call me as soon as she came in, for if Marie flies in, we'll try to get together. Last Sunday, we found a lovely place to swim where the water was so cool and clear. I'm making hot dog rolls now, so we can roast them over a beach fire tomorrow. Every week, we keep saying we'll buy two inner tubes, but we never do. The weeks go so fast here. Before we know it, it will be time to leave for the States or we'll be on our way to Australia. Thursday, we attended a cocktail party on board a Blue Funnel ship and what a time! It poured cats and dogs just before we arrived, but once on board, we were well taken care of. All Singapore really goes in for cocktail parties. Some can be so artificial and then others can be fun. The women seem to set the pace. This afternoon we will see some Sibu people leaving on the big Dutch luxury liner for Genoa. I'm looking forward to seeing the ship and some of the officers we know. Brian and I are toying with the idea of settling in the USA instead of going to Australia. We can't seem to make up our minds. Once living abroad, it isn't bad. I can think of a lot of advantages, but there are disadvantages. I am quite sure we will not be going to England, unless Brian gets a fabulous wage. But some day, maybe when we retire, I would love to live in an English Country cottage by a stream or sea. Did you see the "Holiday" magazine article about London? Brian digested it from cover to cover. I'm beginning to make a folder of places to see, eat, and shop in London and South England."

There had been talk about Brian being transferred to a sister company in Adelaide, Australia, but although there was lots of talk, there was not much action. So, we stopped worrying about it, and we carried on with our life, concerts, plays, cocktail parties on ships, a true social whirl after the laid-back life in Sibu. Although the island of Singapore was not very large, there were all sorts of hidden delights where we least expected them. We notified our friends when we anticipated being in England. Going to England in the winter had its advantages and disadvantages, off season prices and cold weather. With a few long undies, warm coats and sweaters, we would be able to keep warm, popping in here and there for a spot of tea. Brian was thrilled to death over the birthday card Carol Ann sent him. The office staff had to see it. The boss left so Brian and a young fellow, the same age as Brian, ran the lumber business. The officials in London tried to soft soap us into staying, but we wanted to move to Canada.

When our first anniversary passed, I was no longer a bride, but we had a lovely evening celebrating by dancing and walking the waterfront with the waves lashing the beach below and the full moon arising. Brian gave me a lovely "Batik," the special printing of the Indonesians and a finely woven silver pin made in Siam. Before leaving Singapore, I bought a batik dress for traveling. I couldn't resist buying Brian a George Jensen letter opener. We were both interested someday to own a service or two of Danish silver.

For my last month of pregnancy, I was off to the doctor once a week, although I was still running around madly attending cooking classes and going swimming. My Chinese friends thought I was insane driving a car and swimming. Brian played Rugby for the Singapore Cricket Club once or twice a week. One week I sat in the rain watching these over-sized boys knock themselves and the ball around. I found Rugby much more interesting than American football, which I listened to in the afternoons on the Armed Forces Radio Station as well as the World Series. It was always a day or two behind.

Marie McGrath

Chapter 12

The Singapore Riots

On October 27, 1956, I wrote the following letter to my mother about the student riots in Singapore, which started with Chinese students wanting their own way and the government saying no:

"In some of my letters I mentioned these students and the two schools causing the trouble. One of the schools is right next door to our home. Big trouble started Wednesday night when the police and the government warned the students to vacate the schools where they had been camping for 24 hours for two days. By Thursday night, all the students should be off the school property. Brian and I walked over Wednesday evening to see parents driving into the school trying to convince their children to go home, but they refused to obey. They were guarding the gates in front of the school, letting only the parents through. Police guarded the gates on the other side of the school refusing to admit trucks with food or other students. The police wore metal helmets and carried shields on guard all night and throughout the day. Thursday night was the deadline when mobs of people outside the gates started stoning the police. We first thought the noise was from the students yelling slogans at the police, but as it got louder, our cook went to investigate while we stayed in our yard. Dogal, our Malay gardener, climbed the coconut tree and yelled down that the students had just overturned a police wagon and set it on fire. At the Chinese High School next door, three cars were turned over and burnt by the mob. Finally tear gas was used later in the night to get rid of the mob. We turned in early and forgot about the trouble outside. Friday morning about 7 a.m., the police finally broke into the school yard using tear gas to get the stubborn students away from the school. The students were formed into a line outside the school gates and marched two miles down the main road singing Communist songs to familiar tunes such as 'The Battle Hymn of the Republic.'

Tear gas was also being used at the other Chinese High School where the students were throwing desks and chairs at the police. Several students were seriously injured. Mobs of other supporters joined the fight until 3 p.m. when the government called a curfew, initially scheduled to be 22 hours long with people being allowed out only between noon and 2 p.m. This was later reduced to a 12-hour curfew from 6 p.m. to 6 a.m. Reports were on the radio all day and by lunch time things were bad. Brian suggested I spend the afternoon at the Manfield's flats with the rest of the women.

By the time lunch was over, we both decided to take our clothes and spend the night there, locking our house. Bombers, jets, and helicopters were flying low over the place all morning. The helicopters were dropping tear gas on the students and supporters of the riot were entering the school grounds. They were trying to break up the large mobs which formed to set fire to trucks, cars, gas stations, or attack the police. By lunch time, the police were opening fire on the mob that refused to separate when told to do so.

Brian went back to work at 2 p.m., but by 3:30 p.m. he was on his way home. Police stops were all over the town. Machine guns were setup in front of all the government offices, and by now the British Army was in full swing helping to control the mob.

The students were now taking a back seat and organized warfare was going on. The fighting was not just downtown Singapore, but all over the island. Out at the airport, Europeans were attacked, their cars stoned, turned over and set on fire. The airport was officially closed, but things settled down a bit, and flights went back on schedule. The Federation of Malaya has offered to send down 1,000 troops if needed. By 4 a.m. this morning, thirteen Chinese had been killed and over seventy injured. The Duke of Edinburgh is arriving this coming Wednesday, and everyone hopes Singapore will be back to normal. In fact, it is rumored that the government put pressure on the students so this bloody affair would be over before the Duke arrives. The students knew it had to come sooner or later. Brian and I were crossing our fingers all night hoping our little one wouldn't be born. The hospital is way on the other side of town, and we would have to go through some hot places. With the curfew on, anyone outside their home could be fined $1,000.00 or three years in prison or both. Tonight, there is another curfew beginning at 4 p.m., so it looks like all weekend we'll be addressing Christmas cards and writing in our Sarawak scrapbook. Brian had applied for a pass to be out after curfew in case Mark was born. However, the deputy police chief said, 'NO—call an ambulance.' When Brian reminded him that an ambulance had been overturned and set on fire, he relented. Luckily, this was not needed, as the riot was over in a few days before Mark was born on November 1, 1956. Brian had a Rugby game this afternoon, but all gatherings have been cancelled. Movie houses and most eating houses are closed.

Sunday morning a curfew is in affect from 10 a.m. until 6:30 a.m. tomorrow. It will be our first Sunday home since we have been in Singapore. It is such a beautiful morning, lovely soft breeze, warm sun, and clear sky."

The company was still talking about sending Brian to Adelaide but the Australian manager continued to procrastinate. Brian and I talked things over again and decided that, due to the riots, a move was needed, so Brian wrote to MacMillan Bloedel in Vancouver to see if they would offer him a job. MacMillan Bloedel was the company that had hosted Brian and shown him around their operations in May 1955. They agreed to do so, but at a rock bottom wage and a position in the mill.

Marie McGrath—yes, the same Marie who had knocked on our hotel room door at 5 a.m. in Manila while we were on our honeymoon—also flew with Pan American into Singapore. Brian and I had told her that she had an open-ended invitation to stay with us if she ever had enough time. Well, it happened, and Marie ended up at our rented house and was given the spare bedroom which only had a fan, but no air-conditioning. During the middle of the night, Brian heard footsteps in the living room and thought there was an intruder in the house, but it was Marie, who could not sleep, as she was used to air-conditioned hotel rooms. Brian said, "Come and sleep with us. We have a king size bed." So, for the first and only time, Brian was in bed with two women. Marie on one side, a very pregnant me in the middle, and Brian on the other side. What a hoot! Although Brian had played tennis and badminton while in Sibu, there was no way he could get to play Rugby, his favorite sport. When he arrived in Singapore, he joined the odd named Singapore Cricket Club to play the game he loved. In fact, although he is ashamed to admit it, he was playing Rugby when our son Mark was born. In his defense, he says he did rush straight to the hospital from the game—ha!

Mark was born in a superb hospital, Young Berg Memorial Hospital, run by the Seventh Day Adventists who were vegetarians. Consequently, I was being fed croquettes and salads when I was dying for fried chicken. So, one evening Brian took a tiffin carrier (a multi-storied food carrier) full of food that I was craving for, and the idea was that there would be enough food for two. Suffice it to say, I did not see it that way, and Brian ended up feeling distinctly hungry. Brian said Mark was, for the most part, a happy boy, and myself a perfect mother, even though this was my first attempt and a new, different lifestyle evolved. After the birth, I was at my lowest weight for years. Before we knew it, the end of our six month lease on the house was almost over, and Brian started searching for another one and found a beautiful house in the same area where many of our friends lived. The owner worked for Radio Malaya and was going to be moving to Southern Rhodesia (as it was called then) shortly after his return from home leave. The rental period was going to be three to four months, and it would be fine for us as we planned to leave for England, then to the United States and Canada in March.

Dottie and Mark

Chapter 13

Return to America

In March 1957, Brian, Mark, and I flew from Singapore to London on a super Constellation of Quantas Airlines and spent a few weeks in England, which were wonderful. We rented a car and spent a week traveling around seeing the lovely English scenery, staying in a pub, a hotel cum bar, which dated back to the 1600s. We visited at least ten cathedrals, several castles, quaint thatched cottages, and took a day trip to Canterbury. Another day we went to Windsor, Eton, to a concert at Festival Hall and the theater. Our weather was like English summer. Walking in the London shopping area was different; it seemed to be a man's town with rather expensive clothes. Brian and I looked at antique silver, wishing we could buy some. I was afraid the shipping strike might affect our sailing from Southampton because the shoremen wouldn't unhook the ropes. However, we were finally able to sail from Southampton to New York on the original Queen Elizabeth. Since we could only afford the basic tourist class, our quarters were an inside cabin. The winds were fierce, the seas huge, and Brian showed up for only one meal between Le Havre and New York City. The rest of the time he was either bundled up on deck or in the cabin. I was not affected and showed up for every meal.

On my last letter to Carol Ann from my trip, I wrote:

"On April 12, 1957, we arrived in America and spent two days in New York City where Marie Personius and my mother met us at their hotel and drove us to Elmira. It was so good to be back on U.S. soil to see old familiar people and places! Outside of Monticello, our car almost turned over due to the weather, and then about a mile up the road, we got stuck driving on icy roads. It had started to snow farther north. When the car got stuck on the icy road, Brian got out and walked to Monticello to find a garage. He told the owner that we were stuck in the ice. He said, 'You and twenty others.' Brian told him that there was a five-month-old baby in the car, and his attitude changed immediately. He said, 'You will be next when the tow truck gets back.' We were towed to a small hotel where we spent the night. We arrived in Elmira the next day with a foot of snow. Our weather had been terrible—even worse than England's.

Labe came home last weekend, and we drove to Carlisle to visit Grandma, Grandpa and Randy. Brian left for Vancouver because he was starting a new job, and he needed to find us a place to live. He flew from Elmira to Buffalo to Chicago, to Seattle via Denver, and finally from Seattle to Vancouver via Bellingham, Washington. He called me saying Chicago had twenty-degree weather. Since Brian had a long layover in Chicago, I suggested that perhaps he would like to visit one of our classmates, Barbara Tufts, who had contracted polio and was operating out of a wheelchair. Arrangements were made when Brian arrived in Chicago. He hired a taxi, gave Barb's address, only to be asked by the driver, 'Are you sure you want to go there? It is not a good area of the city.'

Brian explained the situation to him and off they went. When they arrived, the taxi driver said, 'When you leave, call for a cab, and don't go down until it arrives.'

Brian had a lovely visit with Barbara, who explained why she lived where she did, which was because of the scarcity of apartment buildings that were wheelchair friendly. Brian didn't have to worry about a taxi back to the airport as Barb said she would drive him in her car, which had been fully equipped with hand controls.

Joyce and Rol, one of her boyfriends, drove down from Auburn on Saturday evening. We had a few drinks and talked at the Mark Twain Hotel. We were driving to Pierces in Elmira Heights when Joyce mentioned that she liked pizza, so off to Morretti's we went for our dinner ordering four different kinds. After that, off to Rustic Gardens at Pendenty, where we giggled. She and Rol reached Auburn around 2 a.m. It was wonderful seeing her again. She brought Mark a darling stuffed poodle dog, so soft and warm, which he loves. Joyce looks and acts the same. She's still Joyce with a few men on the string, of course."

In a letter to Carol Ann from Elmira, I wrote, "Your future looks good. Oh, how I wish you could land a job on the west coast. Maybe, Marie, you and I could get together once in a while. I wish I had the money and the time. I would love to fly down to see you. Mark is behaving as he should. He loves to bite his grandma's nose. He's trying to cut his upper teeth. Last Sunday, Mark was baptized, and the congregation was so surprised to see red hair. Last evening, I spoke on Sarawak at the church for about an hour which really exhausted me. Grandpa called this evening and asked if I would speak in his church on Sunday in Carlisle. I had planned only one more speaking engagement, but there seems to be more popping up. I must get to bed for a bit of sleep before starting out tomorrow for Vancouver to where you need no invitation to visit us."

Thus ends my adventures as a missionary in Borneo. It was a wonderful experience seeing the world, teaching, meeting new friends, and acquainting the students, the Land Dayaks, Sea Dayaks, and other members of the community with Christianity. I never expected to meet and marry the love of my life, Brian Casidy, in that far away land.

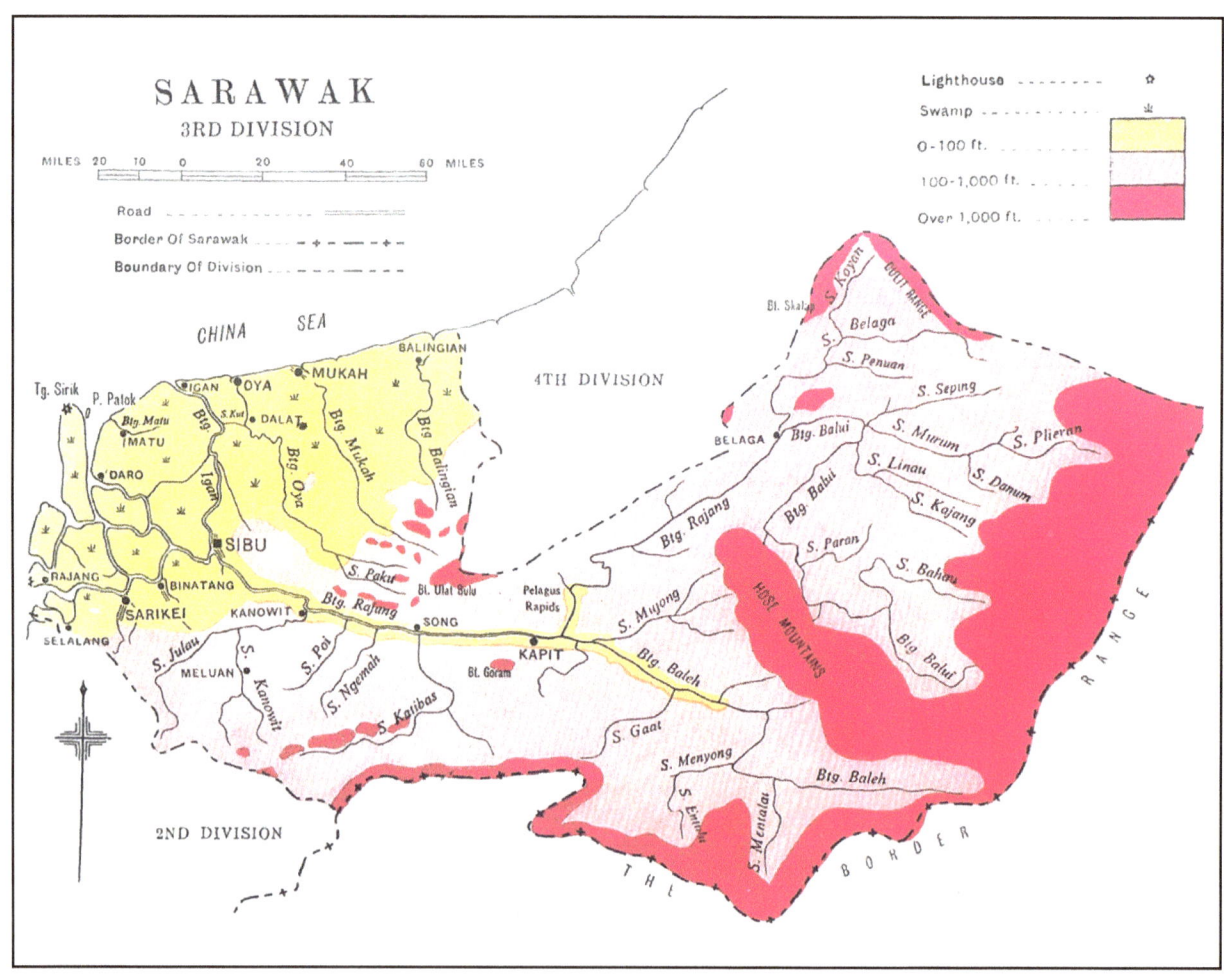

Epilogue

As of this writing, Brian and Dottie Wingert Casidy have had a long, loving, happy married life of over 66 years of which 64 years have been lived in Vancouver, British Columbia where they moved to in 1957. Brian retired early from the lumber business on April 27, 1989, and Dottie remained at home caring for her family, which included three sons: Mark Edwin born on November 1, 1956, in Singapore, Ian Grant born on December 22, 1959, and Blair Andrew born on June 2, 1966, both in Vancouver, B.C. Mark has two boys: Brendan Edwin born on June 4, 1985, who married Ivy on November 16, 2019, and Bryce Donald born February 10, 1988, who married Amanda on April 28, 2018, with two children: Penelope born on April 7, 2019, and Athena born on October 12, 2020; Ian Grant, who married Kerry on May 21, 1988, have two boys: Keegan John born on April 6, 1990, and Patrick Owen born on January 23, 1992; and Blair Andrew, who married Cara on August 14, 2004, have two girls: Sydney Breanna born on November 29, 2004, and Brooke Katherine born on August 10, 2006.

In the summer of 1958, Dottie's mother, Mildred Wingert, and Carol Ann Patterson drove 3,000 miles in Carol Ann's pink Plymouth from Elmira, New York to North Vancouver to visit Brian and Dottie for several weeks when Princess Margaret visited Vancouver. They drove back to New York State via Oregon, San Francisco, Kansas, Cleveland, Buffalo, and Elmira.

In June of 1979, Brian, on a business trip to Japan with Dottie, visited Indonesia, Kuala Lumpur and their old stomping grounds of Singapore and Sarawak. This was a nostalgic trip, as it included visits to Sibu where they were married, and Singapore, where Mark was born.

In mid-March, 2000, Brian and Dottie flew to Kuala Lumpur, Malaysia to stay with their friends, Soo Weng Heng, his wife Ying Ying, and their son Ken. Then they flew to Perth, Australia for five days, to Melbourne, and Apollo Bay, S.W. of Melbourne for a few days. After which, they flew from Melbourne to Kuala Lumpur and Singapore where they met an old friend from 30 years ago in Sarawak.

In their seventies, they left for a 30-day holiday in February via Singapore Airlines from Vancouver to Singapore, stayed in Seoul for a night, not wanting to face a nineteen-hour flight and an arrival in Singapore at 1 a.m. They spent an overnight in Singapore and took an express bus to Kuala Lumpur, where old friends, Soo Weng Heng and Ying Ying, met them. They stayed there four days, took a bus back to Singapore for four days to renew old friendships, and took a five-hour flight to the beautiful city of Perth, Australia.

In January and February of 2005, they celebrated their 50th wedding anniversary by taking a trip to South East Asia. They flew to Hong Kong where they spent their honeymoon in September 1955, spending three days visiting their old haunts. Then, they flew to Singapore where they lived almost a year and where their eldest son, Mark, was born in November 1956. After three days, they took an express bus to Kuala Lumpur, where they were greeted by their Chinese friends. They had a fabulous time there being royally spoiled by Soo and Ying Ying. Afterwards, they flew to Kuching, Sarawak where they spent three days at a beach resort and another three days in the city seeing the fantastic changes that had been made there. Then, they took a long bus drive to Sibu where they had lived for three years, but they hardly recognized it even though they had visited there 20 years ago. However, the church where they were married was still there, but now it was a new concrete, air-conditioned building built on the same site as the old wooden one in the same architectural style as the original one. They took a trip up the river to Kapit in a fast jet boat in two and a half hours, which used to take all day or more in the 1950s. Another fast boat took them down the Rejang River and across the open sea to Kuching for their flight back to Kuala Lumpur, where they stayed two more nights before taking the flight to Hong Kong and on to Vancouver the next day.

In June 2005, Carol Ann Boyles, Joyce Hunter, and Isabel Curry had a mini-college reunion, spending a week with Dottie and Brian in North Vancouver. In May 2006, Brian and Dottie flew to England to visit Brian's sister Barbara, husband, and other relatives before flying to Bordeaux for a three-week holiday in Southwest France. In early November, they took a 16-day trip to China, which included Beijing, Yangtze River Cruise, Shanghai, and other cities. Their last two trips were to East Germany, Austria, and France in 2012 and to England in 2014.

Through the years, Dottie and Carol Ann maintained contact through letters and visits not only in Vancouver, but in Jacksonville and Ocala, Florida.

All in all, Brian and Dottie Casidy have traveled to at least 29 countries, and now they are enjoying their sons, daughters-in-laws, grandchildren, and great grandchildren in Vancouver, British Columbia, Canada.

Brian and Dottie in Vancouver, BC

Resources

1. *Sarawak and Its People*, Wilke & Company Limited, Melbourne, Australia.
2. 1954 Sarawak Annual Report
3. "Borneo Bound—Jungles and Rivers of Sarawak" unpublished manuscript by Brian Casidy
4. Dottie Wingert Casidy's letters to Carol Ann Patterson
5. Photographs taken by Dottie Wingert Casidy
6. Keuka College photograph by Bill Banaszewski, Finger Lakes Images Publishers
7. Photographs taken by Keuka colleagues and Carol Ann Boyles-Jernigan
8. *Rajah Charles Brooke: Monarch of all He Surveyed*, Colin Crisswell, Oxford University Press, Kuala Lumpur, 1978.
9. Wikipedia

Acknowledgments

This book is a collaborative effort between Dottie Wingert Casidy and me. I did my best to remain faithful to her life in Borneo. My 16-year-old granddaughter, Anna Boyles, turned my book in a new direction by encouraging me to have Dottie narrate this book.

My gratitude goes to Brian Casidy, who enhanced the pages of my book by providing his unpublished manuscript, "Borneo Bound: Jungles and Rivers of Sarawak," and other documents. He also reviewed each chapter, provided the pictures of Borneo, and supported me throughout the book's development.

I am also grateful to my son, Scott Patterson Boyles, for his encouragement, helpfulness, and computer expertise in editing each chapter.

About the Author

Carol Ann Patterson Boyles-Jernigan published her first biography, *The Safety Deposit Box Shock*, in 2020. Her professional career encompassed 48 years as an administrator in higher education, directing programs in career development, cooperative education, student organizations, and admissions at Keuka College, Florida State University, and Central Florida Community College (now the College of Central Florida). She is retired from the University of North Florida.

Mrs. Boyles-Jernigan received her BA from Keuka College, the M.Ed and advanced graduate studies from the University of Florida. Her accomplishments are listed in numerous Marquis Publications, including "Who's Who of American Women," "Who's Who In America," and "Who's Who In The World." She is a member of DAR, the Association of University Women (AAUW), and the Winthrop Society. In her retirement, she founded the Jacksonville, FL Christian Women's Job Corps.

Mrs. Boyles-Jernigan lives in Blountville, TN. She may be contacted at molly7804@aol.com.

Also by Carol Ann Patterson Boyles-Jernigan:

The Safety Deposit Box Shock:
Your Secrets Will Find You Out

Coming Soon:

Flying High in the Sky:
A Flight Attendant's Life with Pan American World Airlines Stratocruiser

www.ingramcontent.com/pod-product-compliance
Lightning Source LLC
Chambersburg PA
CBHW061603170426
43196CB00039B/2961